MICHAEL J. HUNT, C.S.P.

College Catholics

A New Counter-Culture

PAULIST PRESS
New York and Mahwah, N.J.

Library of Congress Cataloging-in-Publication Data

Hunt, Michael J., 1941–
    College Catholics : a new counter-culture / by Michael J. Hunt.
      p. cm.
    ISBN 0-8091-3362-8
    1. Church work with students—Catholic Church.   2. Church work with students—United States.   3. Catholic college students—United States—Religious life.   4. Catholic Church—United States—Membership.   5. Hunt, Michael J., 1941–   . I. Title.
BX2347.8.S8H88   1993
259'.24'08822—dc20   92-37378
                                                  CIP

Published by Paulist Press
997 Macarthur Boulevard
Mahwah, New Jersey 07430

Printed and bound in the
United States of America

Contents

Introduction 1

1. Campus Life 11

2. Faith on Campus 26

3. The Catholic Church 37

4. Behavior/Morality/Sexuality 50

5. Parents and Family 65

6. Growth and Decision 80

7. Prayer, Spirituality and the Bible 98

8. Worship 113

9. Catholic Identity 128

10. The Church on Campus: Campus Ministry 139

11. Ten Guidelines to Help Young People
    Deepen Their Faith Life after College 156

With loving gratitude
to

**THE PARISH OF
THE GOOD SHEPHERD**

the only Catholic Parish Church
on Broadway
in New York City

"... from our youth even until now."
Genesis 46:34

Introduction

". . . . These are only hints and guesses,
Hints followed by guesses; and the rest
Is prayer, observance, discipline, thought and action.
The hint half guessed, the gift half understood, is Incarnation."
T.S. Eliot, *Four Quartets*

The rehearsal dinner was winding down. People were making arrangements for rides and getting directions to the church for tomorrow's wedding. I was there in a familiar role— tomorrow afternoon I would be the church's witness, officiating at the marriage of a man and a woman whom I had known all through their college years. Now four years after graduation, they had invited me to celebrate their wedding mass.

On this evening before, I found myself in a corner of the private dining room with the groom and some of his friends from those years at college. Since all of us had known each other well then, and had kept in touch over the years, it was an intimate conversation, full of reminiscences and remembered laughter. At one point the mood turned quite serious, even reflective, when one of the groom's old college teammates asked him to "sum it all up." "What's your philosophical wisdom on the night before you marry Ellen? So, Brian, what do you have to say for yourself tonight?"

Brian looked as if he might have given the question some thought even before it had been asked. "Right now, tonight,"

1

he began, "I feel like I'm closing one circle, and beginning a new one—now with Ellen and the family we hope to have." Brian's old teammate persisted, "So, what's this circle you're closing?" Brian shifted in the chair a bit self-consciously before he said, "At this point in my life, I think I've finally come to love everything that was given to me when I was younger. All the things I had little to say about, and sometimes fought against, are now the most important things in my life. And that really feels like I'm closing the circle."

Brian quickly listed all the things he was born into or acquired early. "I was born here in America, in a large, very Italian family, which is very Catholic. We were lower middle class most of the time I was growing up, so there wasn't a lot of money then. I was a good athlete in school, but also a pretty good student because my parents demanded that. And I've been going out with Ellen basically ever since high school. I often used to wish that I was something else—a WASP, or an atheist—or had easier parents. But now I really love being Catholic, being Italian in America, and the way my parents did it—and I really love Ellen. So I love what I am—really for the first time. That's how I've closed the circle of my life so far. I really love being what I am."

I had known Brian well for eight years, ever since his first month as a freshman in college. I knew the feeling he expressed this night had not always been there, but I could also see that his struggles and anxieties had now resolved themselves in some very basic ways. Brian had closed his circle. It was something you could see in him and, perhaps more surprisingly, he had put it into words that we all understood in the corner of that rehearsal dinner.

On my long drive back to Boston after that wedding, I decided that Brian's description of himself was a measure by which I could understand how college students struggle to grow and find themselves. "Finding yourself" may sound like trite psychological jargon, but it does indicate the importance of coming to terms with and accepting yourself for who you are—and loving that person. Some students, after a stormy passage, are able to do just that, while others never really get there.

Personal integration of all the disparate and conflicting elements within a person creates the wholeness and maturity that most of us can recognize in others, even when we are at a loss to define it. You know it when you see it. Such personal integration has a radiance about it, attracting others and drawing them toward it. We want some of it for ourselves.

At the center of such a person there is a calm self-confidence and balance, an anchor put down deep into the turbulence of life, furnishing security not only to that person but enticing others to depend, perhaps vicariously, on its steadiness. A college student who seems to be on the way to forging this inner identity is always the one the others look to. There will be other qualities—brains, looks, athletic prowess—but when you see a student being genuinely admired, sometimes even imitated, or revered, there is always this personal integration which stitches all the other qualities together into something deeper and more enduring.

Life on an American campus does not make such maturity effortless or obvious. Competing or non-existent values, peer pressure, conformity, ugly forms of competition and an often ruthless social atmosphere make it very painful for most students to find their way. The push and shove of the crowd can be overwhelming, even when the crowd is as small as one's roommates. Most colleges and universities are unable to give students direction because there is no consensus among their leaders about what that direction should be. As a result, there is more than a touch of anarchy on campus, with most administrators settling for the understandable but feeble advice, "Do what feels right for you." Avoiding the contentious issue of "what is right" can be a full-time occupation.

"She really knows what she wants" and "He's really a together person" are the comments I hear students offer about their peers who have a measure of personal integration. They admire people who are self-directed and who are not constantly reinventing themselves to fit in with some ephemeral crowd. Many students often engage in desperate, unhealthy, and illusory behaviors in their efforts to be accepted or popular, when here on campus, as everywhere in life, the surest way to popularity is to be independent of the crowd with its mindless herd instinct. But, as with other people, most college students do not discover that irony for a long time, and for some it is never discovered.

Every fall I watch the freshmen and realize again that they are very young. For the first few months, most of them will never do anything alone. If they need a new toothbrush or an advisor's signature, they will wait for days until they can get someone to go with them. Even the basic need for food is subordinated to the need for at least a small crowd, as every year there are freshmen who become sick, from lack of food, because they won't go to the dining rooms alone. The fear of being alone, or unique, or friendless controls their every action.

Yet every fall I see some freshmen who are different. I see them around campus, by themselves, taking care of their needs, enjoying the company and friendship of others, but fully capable of doing things alone. Knowing the inner fears which usually plague freshmen at a new school, I marvel at their self-direction. Inevitably, these are the kind of students who will introduce themselves, with a self-effacing and refreshing hint that they consider themselves worth knowing.

But change is constant, and by junior or senior year you often see that the frightened freshman has become an independent person who, when he or she needs a new toothbrush or something more significant, goes off and gets it—alone if necessary. But not everyone. A student who was talking with me just a few days before his graduation, bemoaning all the time and opportunities he had wasted over the past four years, put it very well, if sadly: "I'm the type of person who will watch cartoons on TV all day, if everyone around me is doing that."

Religious faith alone does not automatically generate maturity or growth. Sometimes religious behavior can be just another form of crowd pleasing. But on campuses today, religious faith is more often an act of independence, a refusal to be defined by what the crowd has made fashionable. For many of the students I have known, their religious faith is an anchor, a grounding, which permits them to be themselves and to think their own thoughts. Faith is the stitching that binds together the other elements in their life into something that they can wear as their own, and not a garment borrowed from someone else.

Every Sunday night I greet a campus chapel packed with hundreds of students. For fifteen or twenty minutes before mass begins, the chapel is filled with an incredible level of noise, created by the talk and laughter of hundreds of students greeting each other. Visiting parents or students newly arrived from other countries often talk to me about that noise, remarking that they have never been in a church before where people seemed so eager to be there. I explain that it is, in part, an expression of the rambunctious, informal and noisy American youth culture, but that it may also be that they have never before been in a church where the presence of each person represented an act of individual independence.

To the visitor, this student congregation will seem like a joyful mix of friends happy to be together. And so it is. But every Sunday night I also realize that, for each of these students, there was a first, lonely Sunday night. It may have been as early as the first Sunday of freshman year or as late as the final semester as a senior, but each one there came alone the first time, ending up surprised to find that so many others had found the same place. Later they will tell me, now with amusement, about that first Sunday trip to mass on an American campus. They had not told anyone in the dorm where they were going because they didn't want to hear the scorn or ridicule that usually greets religious behavior on campus. They had not expected to find more than a small handful of students huddled in a darkened chapel because it seemed such an *uncool* thing to do. They tell me later about their shock at walking into a packed chapel, of maybe not even finding a seat, and of seeing people they already knew, from their classes, or teams, or even from their dorm. Juniors and seniors, making that trip to Sunday mass for the first time, often tell me, "I've been here three years and I know a lot of these people, but I never knew so many people went to mass."

Later they will come with their friends or meet them just before mass, but every Sunday I remember that, for each of these noisy, laughing students, there was the initial step, the personal act of independence of going alone to a Sunday mass on an American campus.

When I began my first assignment as a college chaplain, the Second Vatican Council had just concluded two years earlier, and all of American society, especially its campuses, was in the midst of that cultural upheaval which is now known collectively as *The Sixties*. I found myself in a church that was undergoing unprecedented change and filled with controversy, serving on a campus which, like all the others, was swirling with waves of unrest over race, academic reform and, above all, the war in Southeast Asia. All these familiar institutions, the church, the university and even the government, teetered under fierce attack and held uncertain futures. Everywhere there was the demand for *relevance*, which usually meant immediate change in some constantly fluctuating direction.

It was an exciting, challenging time to be on campus—a time when we always felt present at the birth of something new. A quarter of a century later, now on a different campus, it appears to me that everything has changed, and nothing has changed. In the intervening years, first at Wayne State University in Detroit, then at Boston University and the University of California at Berkeley, and now at Tufts University, I have watched and read the customary ominous reports in the media about religion and its failures among the young, perhaps especially Catholicism. Yet Sunday after Sunday, on all those campuses, my experience disclosed that large crowds of young Catholics still worshiped regularly in always steady numbers. My random and unscientific observations recently found a kind of verification when the sociologist Andrew Greeley pointed out that the current defection rate among American Catholics is fifteen percent—precisely the same figure it was in 1960 when such measurements were first taken. Everything and nothing had changed in thirty years.

Another sociologist of religion, the Jesuit John A. Coleman, writes about being irked by a "fact" that was displayed as a sight-byte on Ted Koppel's *Nightline*: "By some estimates the Roman Catholic Church has lost twenty-five percent of its members in recent years." Coleman's reaction—"By whose estimate?"—led him to write about the most recent evidence which shows that the Catholic Church loses about 14.5 percent from defection or switching religions, but gains 9.1 percent from conversions, for a net loss of 5.3 percent (John A. Coleman, S.J., "Young Adults: A Look at the Demographics," *Commonweal,* September 14, 1990). Now, at last, the maze of statistics begin to sound close to what I have seen on secular campuses since 1967.

For those in the church who work with college students, as well as for parents and especially for parishes, Coleman challenges the complacency of our timidity and defeatism: "Be warned from the start: What you think you know about young adult Catholics is probably not true, especially if you think that we are worse at retaining them than other religious groups. . . ."

Correcting the prevalent gloomy portraits of Catholicism failing among the young does not mean that we can succumb to an easy optimism. In these pages you will read my observations that many, if not most, of the students who are very active in campus faith communities then drift away after college, failing to find any source of identity with the average American parish. There is considerable evidence that they may well become reaffiliated in time, especially when they marry and begin to have their own children. But the period of years between college graduation and marriage has been steadily lengthening as young people continue with graduate school or early intensive career preparation. Getting married later means that, in this very important life stage, the church is largely absent at a time when young singles may need it most, and at a time when they are freer to serve in the church's mission through volunteering and other activities. The church and young, single Catholics have become strangers to each other. The American parish needs to understand that a significant number of its potential parishioners are right there, unmarried, out of school for the most part, eager and believing, but not being reached by present parish ministries. In this book you will hear my suspicion that it is a problem not so much of structures but of attitude. We have begun to believe all the gloomy media assessments and written off young people because we have been told they have written off religion. You will find no evidence for that defeatist gloom in this book—or at Sunday mass in campus chapels.

The measure of personal integration which Brian articulated to a group of us in a gathering of friends at his rehearsal dinner, and which I recounted at the beginning of this introduction, is real. It happens—maybe more than we think. I have known hundreds of students who bring themselves regularly to Catholic worship because they also know it happens, and if they have not yet experienced it wholly in themselves, they see it in others, and they want it for themselves. It is a perspective, a depth, a profoundly trusting relationship with the universe, a personally liberating access to God and his grace that can be readily discerned in people. It is akin to what the philosophers called the analogy of faith, a wondrous and fulfilling sense of a God at work here, now, in all this. Its absence in contemporary American culture has made us and everything about us reek of superficiality and impermanence, from our marriages to our social reforms. But its absence has made only more acute our desire and craving for its embrace, hoping to find the grounding that will let us believe that "all will be well, and all manner of things will be well."

The sacramental life of Catholicism still draws people to its sacred materialism because it uniquely offers that desired grounding in ways that can be heard, and shared, and spoken, and eaten, and even smelled. It is the most archaic and unmodern religious option around. But it is God, in the bread in your hand, in the person you came with, in the silence, in the sounds and in the noise. God is the point of it all. It is why so many young people on campus go to mass.

This is, perhaps, the great untold story of the Catholic Church in contemporary America, communities of faith growing and thriving in the most unlikely precincts of the modern secular campus. I have heard hundreds of students tell me their own stories of the journey of faith. In these pages I want to tell you about these students. Some are the stories of faith deepened, some of faith lost or never found; some are stories of students who grew into very impressive people, some of students who lost their way. They have made me think and rethink everything I thought I ever knew, in ways that continue to astound me. From their stories I have tried to derive some meaning, some insight, some direction, always discovering the near impossibility of drawing any confident conclusions about their time in life. But there is the confidence that I am at least witnessing the future, unfolding in each one of their journeys. Join me then, in these pages, as we unravel the future of a love that is "ever ancient, yet ever new."

A Note to the Reader: The stories of students which I tell in this book are all real but anonymous. Some are composites of many stories and some are told in ways which make recognition impossible, but they are all stories which I have known and shared.

1

Campus Life

CONTRADICTIONS

Each semester I invite students to join a group that meets together in my office for an hour once a week. The students set the topics for discussion, which may be any issue or problem that a member of the group wants to bring up. I am there mostly to get it going, sometimes to keep it on track, and to end it after one hour. The group doesn't have a formal name, but, from the topics which are frequently brought up, it is often called *The Personal Issues Group*. Problems in families or in boyfriend/girlfriend relationships, life on campus, and career decisions are often talked about. Usually the atmosphere is a bit guarded.

But on this Monday, everyone was talking, sometimes all at once. A sophomore woman had just spent ten minutes vividly describing the horrors of living in her dorm. She was fed up and dispirited. On some weekend mornings the stench of vomit in the bathrooms from drunken revelers of the previous night is so repulsive that she has to roam through other dorms on campus looking for a bathroom where she can take a shower without getting sick herself from the smell. But this past weekend pushed her close to the edge, when students on her floor held a party during which they played a game in the corridor which consisted of rapidly drinking cans of beer and then spinning yourself around as quickly as possible. The first one to throw up was the winner, with second and third and fourth places being awarded on the same basis. Next morning, students who were able to get up had to put on rainboots or snowboots to walk though the mess in the corridor. It was still there this morning, two days later.

As this student laces the telling of her woes with caustic references to "here at an elite school" and "this is costing twenty thousand a year," her story unleashes a torrent of similar episodes in other dorms. But another sophomore, a young man studying engineering, cautions them about the futility of complaining to the authorities, by recounting his freshman year experience with a roommate who was constantly smoking pot in their room. When he complained, he was told to "just talk it over with your roommate and try to find a compromise solution." Cynically he wonders if they should have set specific hours when pot smoking was allowed. A senior woman tells of being slapped around by a male student when she declined his sexual overtures at a campus party. Some in the group insist that she should have brought formal charges against him, but she explains that he had been drinking quite a bit and so maybe he really didn't know what he was doing. "That's no excuse," insists a woman in the group, but others tended to view his drinking as an extenuating circumstance, "as long as she wasn't hurt too badly." The woman who had been slapped around seems to agree, and besides, she says, she wasn't really hurt so badly.

My only intervention in the discussion was a question as we ended: "Does anybody consider these things normal?" I was told, "No, but that's what happens. And there's nothing you can really do about it."

A few days later on campus, with visions of the dormitory corridor still fresh in my mind, I run into a colleague, an irreverent and astute observer of campus happenings, who describes himself as a "very curious agnostic." He regales me with a recent experience when he gave a talk to a local community group which displayed spirited indignation about what they perceived was happening on campuses. "I told them all about you Catholics," he tells me, "without ever mentioning the word *Catholic*. I told these folks that, while some awful things surely occurred on campus, they should also know that, on this campus, the largest voluntary, not-for-credit gathering of students that takes place on a regular basis is a weekly meeting to commemorate an act of unselfish love." Nudging me with his elbow, he confides, "Of course, I was referring to that huge crowd of students that show up for your Catholic mass."

Those of us who serve on campuses become so accustomed to these radically conflicting experiences that we soon become oblivious to how contradictory they are. Like other institutions in our society, the American campus, depending on how you slice it and what slice you're presently looking at, can be either a fairly crude and unmanageable locale, or a fascinating hub of learning and even of deep religious faith. It's a bewildering spectrum of all these elements. And we need to look at all of them.

THE AMERICAN CAMPUS

American colleges and universities are among the best in the world, drawing students here from every continent. They are also unparalleled among the world's institutions of higher learning, reflecting, as they do, the uniquely American aspiration to provide educational opportunities and advancement for a broad spectrum of our society. No other society has assumed such an ambitious venture. As a result, higher education here is supported by large sums of public funds, directly to the state universities and, indirectly, to the private institutions. Even with the cut-backs of recent years, the role of the university, in enabling the children of the lower economic classes to reach better and more productive lives, remains largely unquestioned. "Go to college, you'll get a better job" is an American truism.

Colleges and universities have tried to accelerate their own contributions to these societal goals by expanding admissions procedures, through affirmative action and diversity strategies, in order to attract and retain young people from groups previously under-represented in the university population: African-Americans, Hispanics, women, the disabled and other groups. Some critics claim that these efforts have been superficial and call for more radical measures of minority inclusion. Yet others maintain that these affirmative action admissions policies have lowered the standards of American education. But, whatever one thinks of these raging controversies, it is clear that higher education in this country, much more than anywhere else, closely mirrors the larger society, with its tensions and conflicts. Students on an American campus in the 1990s come from all classes, from all social and economic backgrounds.

As would be appropriate for a society as differentiated as ours, colleges and universities range in character from huge state-sponsored mega-campuses like Berkeley and the University of Michigan, to the private but powerful like Harvard and Stanford, to the religiously-based like Notre Dame and Southern Methodist, to the small and the sectarian like Bob Jones and Liberty, not to even mention thousands of community and junior colleges.

Who pays for all this? Nobody really knows. While the taxpayer obviously picks up a large chunk of the bill, students are also financed by a complex combination of sources, including parents, of course, but also by bank and government loans, by public and private scholarships for academic or athletic skills, by direct financial aid from wealthier schools, and, as always, by working themselves. At publicly financed institutions, like Wayne State and Berkeley, I was not surprised to know students from all economic backgrounds, but here at Tufts, one of the most expensive private schools in the nation, I still meet students whose fathers are delivery truck drivers or whose mothers are single parents living on public assistance. Although colleges are organized for a four year program leading to a bachelor's degree, the average student takes five years to finish the degree, because students take time off or attend only part-time, mostly to work and save some money to pay the tuition bills.

It would still be misleading to say too easily that, in America of the 1990s, anyone who wants to go to college can do it, but it is more important to say that no students should rule themselves out of a college degree just because they don't have the tuition in the bank. It can be done.

The net result of all this is that nearly every segment of our society is present on campus, urging and advocating their perspectives and ambitions. This mixture alone might be worth the tuition in terms of sheer education, and many universities actively pursue more diverse student bodies for just that educational objective.

Yet, while you will find some reflection of every part of American society on campus, there is still a measure of insularity and unreality about academic life. College students are still sheltered in many ways from grimmer realities. If you get sick, there's a health service. Special police usually patrol the campus. In your dormitory dining room, someone prepares your meals. In a consumer society, college officials view parents and students as customers and make strenuous efforts to package their product attractively. The competition for students is very strong among all institutions, making it a buyers' market. Not surprisingly, students routinely distinguish their campus environment from what they call the "real world."

COMPLETE AND TOTAL FREEDOM

Paramount among campus unrealities is the level of freedom students suddenly discover as soon as their parents drop them off on that first day as freshmen. Any rules, restrictions, and inhibitions which may have plagued their teenage years at home disappear as quickly as their parents' car or van departs the campus. That first freshman night on campus can be an adolescent's dream fulfilled. Their bedrooms are now a few paces removed, in the same building, from the bedrooms of dozens of potential sexual encounters. The local legal restrictions about drinking age, or the possession of other drugs, rarely matter on the third floor of a dormitory. There will be exams and papers, but no one bothers you about them—until, of course, later when they're due. Parents and school administrators who once seemed to be everywhere, always watching, are now present mostly at the other end of a telephone, or in a 9 to 5 office on another side of the campus. You have to tell your parents something about your new life on campus, but, as you quickly realize, now you are the editor-in-chief of all the information that flows their way. It's time to party!

During the campus turmoil of the 1960s, most colleges gladly surrendered one of the bulwarks of their power, as they divested themselves of the role *in loco parentis.* "It is not our responsibility," they all said at once, "to play the role of the parent for these students. They're old enough. They're on their own." It was a clean, total solution to the breakdown of any consensus about right behavior, and it changed the American campus overnight. Coed dorms, unregulated hours, meager law enforcement, and less structured academic requirements—all happened at once. Where once there were limits to visiting hours by members of the opposite sex, today administrators will likely facilitate a discussion about how to react when your roommate has her boyfriend over every night, sleeping with her in the bed a few feet from your own. "No rigid right or wrong answers, please, let's just talk it out!"

Today, many administrators, who would never let the antediluvian words *in loco parentis* pass their lips, are trying to reclaim some of that regulatory power because there are serious problems, and many of the consumers are complaining. After many years of not interfering with student behavior, college administrators are now under intense pressure, from trustees, parents, alumni and government, to deal with problems of widespread alcohol and drug abuse, date and acquaintance rape, sexually transmitted diseases, racial and ethnic conflicts and even violence on campus. The new rules now being devised have put the American campus right back in the center of the public controversy which it usually endeavors to avoid.

There's no going back. The American campus will have to devise new ways of getting control of itself and its problems. But such a process, if it is to be worthwhile, needs to face the root miscalculation of the recent experiments: all of us grossly overestimated the emotional and social maturity of American eighteen year olds. They are simply not ready to be so totally on their own. The evidence of this miscalculation is apparent from a glance at any college newspaper which will devote much of its campus coverage to what older newspapers used to call the "Police Blotter," accounts of illegal and anti-social behavior by students. Another measure, commonly apparent to me at least, is a comparison of American students with their classmates from other countries. International students are generally three years more mature than an American student of the same age.

Some, who share my sense of how very young American students tend to be, point to our comparative affluence and how it allows parents and schools to purchase so much protection to shelter youth from the harsher things in life. But my experience tells me that this immaturity cuts across economic lines. Strangely for a supposedly egalitarian society, young people come to college accustomed to being taken care of, whether by parents, teachers and coaches, or by servants who clean up after them, or by social workers in a welfare agency. Other societies divide themselves into children and adults, with an eighteen year old clearly expected to be in the latter category. We have invented the stage-in-between, "the teenage or adolescent stage," and created whole industries to take care of them and to cater to their needs. They come to college, looking for the new set of care-givers, unprepared to live on their own or think for themselves. In a further irony, in societies where the eighteen year old is more mature, students generally live at home with their families while attending a university, whereas we, who haven't required adult behavior of our teenagers, send them off to live hundreds or thousands of miles away from home, in settings where supervision or accountability is largely non-existent.

COMMON SENSE, COMMON WORDS

Ted Koppell was winding down his *Nightline* interview with a Middle East arms merchant late one night when my phone rang. It was the parent of a newly arrived freshman calling to see if I could help. He explained that we had met briefly at the chaplains' reception on the day the new students arrived. Now five days later, his son Ed kept calling to say he wanted his parents to come and take him home. Each time he called, Ed would break down and start crying. Two days before a member of the dormitory staff had noticed there was something wrong with Ed and brought him to the counseling center on campus where a psychologist tried to determine if he was suicidal. As Ed had tearfully explained to his parents, "I don't want to kill myself. I just want to come home."

Now, after midnight, on the phone, his father asked me if I would talk with Ed. "Of course," I said, but explained my personal policy about not being the go-between with parents and students. I suggested to the father that the next time he talked to Ed, he mention that he had talked with me and that I said I would be glad to talk with Ed, if Ed wanted to talk. Twenty minutes later Ed himself called me and asked if he could talk with me—right now. And so in another twenty minutes I sat on a bench by the student center and listened as Ed told me how awful he felt since coming to school. He missed his family and his friends, and now everyone here at school thought he was about to kill himself. He just wanted to go home. I asked him if he thought he might be homesick—a word that stopped him cold.

Ed became very quiet, scanning his inner thoughts for a moment. "Do kids get homesick at college?" he asked. "Sure they do, all the time," I assured him, "but of course nobody would ever admit it, or at least would never use the word 'homesick.'" Ed shook his head, "It's kind of embarrassing to say it," he went on, "but I think that's what's wrong. I'm just homesick right now." The mood has lightened considerably, and we talked about his dorm, his classes and what he wanted to study. As we parted, Ed thanked me for coming over to talk, assuring me that his homesickness probably wasn't too serious because you usually got over it in a few days.

Apparently so. His father called me a day or so later,

profusely apologizing for having disturbed me so late the previous night. "Ed apparently just had a bad case of being homesick," he said, "Nothing serious enough for counseling. He sounds much better today."

Ed's problem had been that his very common malady of homesickness was almost turned into something incredibly and unnecessarily complicated. Fortunately, as he had told me, it passed and he probably doesn't remember it anymore. But complicating ordinary things is one of the perennial flaws of the academic environment. Students, especially freshman but all of them as well, do get homesick, feel embarrassed, make mistakes, wonder if they're up to it, worry about making friends. In those moments, knowing that the feeling is ordinary, common, widespread can be the most effective therapy.

THE COMPETITION

Competition is the American way. It's the proven way to get results, and it's how young people get into college in the first place. There is never just one brand of food or appliance in an American store. We get to pick and choose, rewarding the best product with our purchase, providing higher profits for the producer of the better product. The ones which cannot compete for our favor are eventually removed from the shelves and quickly forgotten. The competitive free market system has undoubtedly been a boon for most of us.

From a young age, college bound children are part of an equally competitive process in which, like the supermarket shelves, there are winners and losers. It may seem a bit extreme, but not inconsistent, to learn that sophisticated parents are already engaged in increasingly fierce competition to get their toddlers into the right kindergarten so they can grow up and get into schools like Yale or Stanford, places where the winners end up. Even with broader and more inclusive admissions programs, getting into the right college is a matter of a relentless competition, no less so because the terms of competition may now include criteria of race and gender.

Nearly every aspect of a young person's life feeds into the great competition laden with lifelong consequences: grades, athletic abilities, extra-curricular activities, travel, family connections with the college, and the personality that comes across in the interview. In the end, only a relatively small number will be able to enter the very elite colleges, with the rest settling for the merely good schools.

The competitive process, with its winners and losers, inevitably creates feelings of inferiority, even among those who actually win. The *Harvard-mistake syndrome*, not at all limited to that prestigious institution, accurately describes the inner doubts of the student who, though accepted at a top school, still thinks a mistake was made in the admissions office and that he or she does not really deserve to be there. It is so often announced that the stakes are very high and that the demands will be very strenuous. As a result, most students will interiorize feelings of inadequacy, incompetence and unimportance, no matter how good they look on paper. The inner fear of failure is always just below the surface.

Competition is never ending. Once the student becomes part of a social group of friends and roommates, peer competition is always the tacit dynamic of the group. "Who's the best?" and "Who has the most?" are the questions that underlie conversations about grades, families, boyfriends/girlfriends or standing on campus. It never ends. Some students compete by talking incessantly about their accomplishments and possessions, even though everyone else can see they are trying to convince themselves of something they don't quite believe, and they never seem to be able to quiet their feelings of insecurity with all their talk. Yet other students, no more secure about themselves, finding the whole process repulsive, just clam up and reveal almost nothing about themselves. They may well be friendly and outgoing, knowing hundreds of other students, but no one knows much about them, about their families, their grades, or their aspirations.

RELATIONSHIPS

Students conceal themselves from one another because they are always in competition with each other. And so they are driven to find someone they can trust, someone who will accept them completely. Finding that someone can become an almost desperate search for college students. They call these connections *relationships*. Boy-meets-girl is deliverance, at least for a while, from the unrelieved pressures of competition. Sexual desire and fulfillment may be the accepted explanation of these relationships, but the intensity of their companionship, along with the explosiveness of their predictable break-ups, can only be understood in the profound need these young people have for at least one other person who will relieve them of the remorseless struggle for acceptance and performance which competition requires of them. Later we will discuss the sexual behavior and morality prevalent among college students, but first it is important to see how incessant competition, and a desire to be rescued from it, drives the frenzy for such intense relationships in the first place.

Marriage, or even long term partnership, is not even on the horizon for these rigorously exclusive and private relationships. They are only immediate, for the moment. A student will enter into an emotionally compelling relationship three weeks before leaving for a year abroad, knowing full well that the relationship will not survive the time and distance, because the need is now, this weekend. Words of undying love and intimate secrets are shared without time-consuming preliminaries. "I met someone," a student will tell me, "and we're really close and good for each other." I don't ask "How long ago did you meet?" because, given the calendar we live on, I know that it was a week, a month at most. I know that now, as always, two nineteen or twenty year old students are seeking in each other, and only from each other, the resolution of all their feelings of inadequacy, homesickness, fear of failure, unworthiness and just sheer fear itself. Such a relationship is bound to be bitterly disappointing. It will break up as quickly as it became so intense, usually because one of them will find someone else who seems to be better, for the moment, at alleviating the raw feelings. There will be harsh pain and depression for while, until each finds a new relationship which appears to heal that pain.

The unreality of these relationships is impressed on me by the contrast of those students, usually very few in number, who explain to me that they have deliberately opted out of the campus frenzy for relationships. Sometimes they rely on the ruse of the purposely exaggerated boyfriend/girlfriend back home, or they direct their social activity to a group. They have figured it out, and decided they don't need the emotional turmoil which consumes their friends. Most often such students satisfy many of their emotional needs within their families, a rare experience in the scattered modern American family.

WHAT THEY WANT IS WHAT THEY NEED

On any campus, the days of September are the most memorable. The cooler weather invigorates and seems to unleash new energy. You don't have to be on a Big Ten cam-

pus to feel football in the air. And it is always in September
that everything seems new and fresh. In fact, about twenty-
five percent of the students are new. The university is really
starting life all over again and the campus pulses with new life
everywhere. In September the vitality of the campus, its librar-
ies, classrooms and laboratories, is extraordinary. People like
myself who have been on campus for many years feel reborn
and maybe, in our illusions, young again.

The excitement of autumn does wear off in the months
ahead, but the role of the university in the lives of its students, and in the whole society, is a most remarkable and
renewable resource. Students become proficient in the arts;
some become engineers and scientists—right before your
eyes. You see it happen.

Thumb through the course catalogue of a modern American college or university. It is an intimidating experience,
glancing at pages of the sophisticated and complex courses
that describe the world in which students live and work.
Even a person who was well educated twenty or thirty years
ago will marvel at what students now learn in the sciences, in
technology and in the arts. But it is also deceiving. Students
are like the rest of people, with the same emotions, fears and
escape mechanisms. They are poorly served by those who
make the student experience too unique. Parents, administrators, counselors, and chaplains do much better when they
offer life experience and its truths to students who, in fact,
are longing for such wisdom.

The contemporary American campus is the engine of a
yet unimagined future, but its inhabitants are people who
usually detect the unreality of much of their environment.
That is why, on campus, they refer to everything off-campus
as the *real world*. Astonishing things are discovered in campus laboratories and in literature seminars, but no one has
ever found the way to live out their life in such places. Stu-

dents intuitively know that the meaning of life and its secrets reside elsewhere, in people who have lived in ways that seem worthwhile. They want to know how you do that in your life. That's what they're asking from us.

Is anybody listening?

2

Faith on Campus

"All week I've felt like a pornographer," he tells me, "or like someone with a terrible secret." Phil is recounting his experiences in the week since he spoke to the Catholic student community about his own faith life. He is a well-known student, articulate, intelligent, a varsity baseball player and very witty. Now he is laughing at the reactions he's being getting all week to his talk last Sunday night. For the past semester a number of students have been speaking briefly at the end of mass about their experience of being a Catholic. Phil's talk last week had ended with his revelation that, every night for a few minutes, he actually talked things out with God, reviewing the events of the day that was ending and asking God to be with him tomorrow. Now, all week, students who heard him speak last week have been coming up to him and telling him things like, "I'm glad you said that thing about your prayer at night, because I do the same thing." The reason he jokingly says it makes him feel like a pornographer is that people take him aside to whisper this message in total privacy, looking around to make sure no one is listening.

"I didn't think it was such a big deal," he tells me, "and I never realized that people would treat a bit of prayer like a big secret." However, the secret part doesn't surprise me.

The students who told Phil how much they identified

with his revelation about his prayer life are, like most of us, influenced by cultural factors which have increasingly confined religious expressions to the private, personal realm and which suggest that it is somehow inappropriate or offensive to speak publicly about such matters. In addition, students live in a climate, to which they themselves contribute, that enjoys heaping scorn and ridicule on sacred or traditional customs. A student who turns to prayer as part of a daily experience would be relieved to have that experience validated by hearing another student speak about it in public. At the same time, students who pray would want their privacy protected from scoffing or ridicule, especially when their practice of prayer is important to them.

Accepted notions in academic circles, to which students are only erratically attentive, would think it very *uncool* to be religious in any overt sense. And in many of these circles, candor about practicing Catholicism could provoke hostility. On campus it is fashionable to talk about religion as a weakness which is fine for those who need it but all the while proclaiming one's self-reliance. Somewhat acceptable is the personal redefining of religious tradition, as in "I have spiritual values" or "I have faith but not for institutional religion."

Students who are hesitant to be very public about their religious practices are understandably reacting to the hostility toward religion that characterizes the secularist mentality which frequently predominates in the university. In American society, beyond the university, such restraint about religion, or God, or prayer is obviously unnecessary. Presidents and other major public figures in this society do not hesitate to speak about their faith or their need for prayer. In most cases the reaction is favorable and supportive. But on many campuses, a secularist ideology has been enshrined which treats religion as a vestige of the past and which, in the interest of diminishing divisions among students, consigns religion to the innocuous private sphere. This treatment of religion is one of the many factors that illustrate the insularity of the campus from the broader American society which is, in fact, a very religious society.

Yet even on campus, secularism is only a facade which, upon closer inspection, does not adequately describe the behavior of people in the campus community, especially students. In many of the departments at the universities—the sciences, engineering, and technology, for example—there is little evidence of this secularist dismissal of religion. In some of the liberal arts it does appear to be dominant where it is mixed with other ideologies that regard religion as a regressive force in society. The mood or atmosphere on many campuses, in the school media, on faculty committees and among many administrators, shares this secularist view, largely because these liberal arts departments understandably supply the most vocal and active members of a university community.

If you spend a few days on a campus, soaking up the atmosphere of the place, you would easily and quickly conclude that it is a very advanced, very modernistic place in which religion is largely non-existent.

Unless your visit included a stop at Sunday mass!

In fact, if you had designed your visit to include the religious groups on campus, you might be surprised that the ones which attract the largest numbers of students are those which do not accommodate to the prevailing secularist pattern which you would have probably sensed all over the campus. In many parts of the country you would discover large and spirited evangelical and fundamentalist Christian congregations of students. In some parts of the country you would also see smaller but very cohesive Eastern Orthodox student groups. At some schools you would be struck by the growing number of observant, orthodox Jewish students. Nearly everywhere you would find large numbers of Catholic students attending church. In a recent sampling of Catholic chaplains at many different schools, I discovered that every one of them said that the Catholic worship on campus was the "largest *by far*" of all worship services.

PERCEPTIONS

"It doesn't make sense to me," she tells me as she interviews me for a paper she is writing for a sociology class. Gail, a senior, came from a religious family but abandoned all religion when she was still in high school. Understandably concluding that her own experience was fairly typical of most college students, she set out to write a research paper on how college students abandon traditional religions. None of her friends, she tells me, are religious anymore, so she purposely attended all the religious services held on campus. One denomination where she expected to find a significant number of students, because it was the most "liberal and up-to-date," surprised her when there were only six students at the Sunday service. But when a Baptist student invited her to come along with some students who attended a church near the campus on Sundays, she was amazed to find about seventy-five of her fellow students in attendance at a service which focused on the literal interpretation of the Bible. Last Sunday, when she looked in on the Catholic mass in the campus chapel, she was even more surprised to see hundreds of students there. After that mass she had introduced herself and asked if she could interview me later in the week for her sociology paper.

Now, she tells me, she will have to redo completely the original thesis of her paper. She laughs as she tells me that, in her mind at least, she had already written the conclusion of her paper: traditional religions are dying out because young people no longer attend their services. I ask her what her new conclusion will be. "Well," she says, "the religions that go against the grain of what's accepted on campus are the ones that are attracting people." She asks if this is a new phenomenon. But I tell her that I've been on different campuses for nearly twenty years and that has always been the case, at least in my experience. She is not tempted to take another look at her own religious background, but she is open-minded and is excited about discovering something new. She worries, though, about whether her professor, whom she describes as "very modern in her attitude toward religion," is going to like her paper with its new conclusion.

At times I am as mystified as Gail by the large response to Catholic worship. Catholic chaplains at other schools tell me they are also often surprised. The Catholic Church, after all, has refused to attune its teachings to the sexual revolution. Everyone knows that it is strongly opposed to abortion. Women cannot become priests. The pope is usually portrayed in the media as a hopeless anachronism. There are public scandals about the behavior of some priests. At times the church seems hopelessly caught in a morass of discord and controversy. Yet students find their way to Catholic worship.

WHY?

Every few years I ask the students who attend mass to fill out a brief questionnaire. One question always is: *What are the reasons some of your friends give for no longer attending mass?* They always list the factors I mentioned a few minutes ago but they often add their own skepticism about whether these are their friends' real reasons, citing less intellectual issues such as "they just don't do anything unless they have to." But when asked to give reasons for their own attendance, these students are nearly unanimous in pointing to God and their relationship with God as their primary reasons for going to mass.

As Gail did, they perceive the Catholic Church as "going against the grain" of what's accepted on campus, and surely at times going against the grain of their own behavior. But isn't that the whole point of worship?—being pulled or stretched to become more than you are already? Upon reflection, I can understand that attending a worship service, which endorsed or approved the way I am now, would have little effect on me, and surely would lose its power to challenge me or to remind me of what I could be.

Groucho Marx used to say that he would never join a club that would have him as a member. A religious variation of that is at work here. Few will follow a religion which merely accepts what they are right now. An important element in all transcendent religion is the hope, not just for a better after-life, but for a fuller and deeper prospect for oneself in this life. Even when I am painfully conscious of my failure to live up to Catholic ideals in my life, Catholic worship tells me there is forgiveness, and there is more—more to me and more to life yet to come. The pop psychology of our culture constantly tells us "I'm OK, you're OK," but most of us don't believe that, and most of us certainly don't want to settle for that. Catholic worship assures me that I am on a journey—the present moment is only one stage—and there is always more to come. Young people are notoriously unhappy with who they are and, perhaps more than the rest of us, resonate with the hope of a future yet to come. They find it very truthful to their own experience to pray for the coming of a future kingdom.

KNOWLEDGE OF FAITH

A few years ago, at the last mass of the school year, I told students that I had been truly shocked by only one thing in the class that was about to graduate. I could see all their heads pick up quickly to see if I was going to reveal some knowledge of shocking sexual behavior. My biggest shock, I told them, was to discover that many of them did not know what happened in 1492. My shock grew massive when, at the refreshments after mass, many of them said to me, "So, what did happen in 1492?" Some even took the time to explain that my question was really unfair since dates are not important anymore.

Many studies have been published in recent years about the cultural illiteracy of young people, including those who are students at the best universities. For those of us who did learn dates or can identify the author of *The Canterbury Tales* or do some math without a calculator, it is a cause of some alarm.

It is also true of their religious knowledge. From similar surveys I have done in a course which I teach in the religion department, I know that many of those hundreds of students at mass cannot cite a major difference between Protestants and Catholics, or explain how a pope is chosen, or name the four gospels, or mention one important result of the Second Vatican Council or even when it took place. With some exceptions, today's college student has had a religious education, whether in Catholic schools or in parish CCD, which followed methods of much secular education. Emphasis was on themes, experience, group interaction, and especially feelings. One very positive result is that young people in the church now have grown up with positive images of God as loving and forgiving. But they want more. Already they are having some of those life experiences of failure and disappointment which drive people to search more deeply for God and for meaning. That nice God who made the rainbows and friends and warm sunny days is not sufficient when you are betrayed by someone you loved or when you have to face a failure that may shape your future years. The book of Job, the psalms that are bitter and plaintive, and even the passion of the Lord were largely deemphasized in their religious education along with the rote memorization and lists of venial sins.

By the time they reach college, most young people have had to cope with some tragedy, often the suicide or fatal accident of a classmate, and they already know some older people whose faith has given them immeasurable strength in dealing with loss or illness. They want that more comprehensive faith for themselves. They even suspect that this may involve knowing the history, without the dates of course, of those who have gone before them in the faith. Not surprisingly, among the elements of Catholicism that most spark their interest are *the Saints*. Surprise!

Recently the university where I serve received a grant from the Lily Foundation to study the future of its religion department and, after consulting with religion departments at many similar universities, discovered that everywhere the enrollment in religion courses on campus has been increasing dramatically. While this academic interest in religion is clearly not the same as religious practice, it does indicate the desire for more substantial and intellectually satisfying understanding of religion among a range of students. When I offer a course on Catholicism on our campus, students whom I see at mass every Sunday frequently tell me they want to take this course because "I really love my religion but now I would like to learn *something* about it."

The low estate of the religious education of the young must be placed in the context of overall education, but it is also an opportunity for those who conduct ministry on campus to meet this need in sermons and seminars and, where possible, through university courses.

IT IS GOD

I was the only Catholic on a panel of campus ministers at a workshop sponsored by a major Protestant denomination. Toward the end of the workshop, a Protestant chaplain at another college directed a series of questions at the panel about the Catholic ministry on college campuses. He wanted to know why, on his campus as on many others, so many students showed up for Catholic mass in comparison with other religious services. He wondered if the Catholic Church was so successful in instilling a sense of obligation in people when they were young that it survived even what he called the "hostile secular world of the university." And he added his opinion that such a sense of obligation was not a bad idea in a world where so few obligations were tended to seriously.

My first response, a bit flippant, was to ask in return if he knew very many eighteen to twenty-two year olds who did things largely out of a sense of obligation, unless they were being monitored. The laughter in this audience of experienced campus ministers indicated that most of them, like me, did not attach much weight to the "sense of obligation" among students. More seriously, I explained what I had learned from regular surveys of students who do practice Catholicism, especially when asked why they went to church. As I said earlier, God was the near unanimous answer. Surely, I added, the very notion of God implies some obligation, but I think the answer—God—should be taken at face value. In the case of Catholicism and its worship, there is never any question about God being the point of it all. We don't publish sermon topics or emphasize guest speakers. The music is often very routine. We leave little ambiguity about the point of the mass. It is God.

All religion is about God. But religion is also about being human, about human behavior and human aspirations. The divine and the human are, by definition, distinct realities, and in religion one is often lost because of the emphasis that is given to the other. It is always a balancing act. For a long stretch of human history, religion was virtually the only source of guidance about human behavior. Today norms about human behavior also come from movements which are not strictly religious in their origin, e.g. ecology and racial justice. If religion devotes itself almost exclusively to the human and to human fulfillment, it often appears to have lost its sense of transcendence. Much of contemporary religion, perhaps unfairly, is perceived, especially by young people, as a kind of alternative but not very distinctive humanism.

But religion which continues to give paramount place to God and his worship meets people at a place in their lives that is untouched by any other source. Religious worship must always grow out of the human experience but it cannot remain there, if it is to be worship. God is such an overpowering concept for most of us that worship must provide us with some reliable medium for encountering him. Belief in God is rarely something which can be sustained or deepened by individuals alone or without a community with a history of faith.

The simple reality remains that on college campuses, as in the whole society, people turn most often and in much greater numbers to those forms of religion which convey the sense of transcendence and whose worship makes that accessible. People with a highly secularized view of reality always find this surprising, even unbelievable, precisely because secularism has devalued the transcendent dimensions of religion, while retaining some of its more general moral precepts. Furthermore, secularists in our time commit the elementary error of assuming that their theories accurately describe the great majority of people in the last years of the twentieth century. But, in truth, while much of the elite class in society may be highly secularized, most people are not. Every study of American society continues to reveal that about ninety-four percent of the people believe in God, with a slightly higher percentage saying they pray (some non-believers also pray occasionally). We do not live in a highly secular society.

On the American campus, the figures for belief and prayer are no doubt a bit different, especially since students like to experiment with various forms of belief and unbelief. But, like *the real world*, the campus community is not a secular society. The desire to know God and to be nourished by God can be observed on every campus. Some might even say that it is rampant.

3

The Catholic Church

QUESTIONS NOT ASKED

Sometimes you don't ask the question that is really on your mind.

She was so angry that I could only be grateful her anger wasn't directed toward me. Spread out on my desk was the annual yearbook, opened to the pages devoted to the religious organizations on campus. The text relating to the Catholic community was a satirical and irreverent description of the mass. She demanded to know what could be done about it. I explained that, months earlier, the yearbook staff had requested a short sketch about the Catholic community, but the yearbook editors had obviously decided to substitute their own rather crude parody of Catholic worship.

Elaine was graduating next month, but this was the first time in four years that we had met each other. She explained that, while she hadn't been to a Catholic service since her confirmation six or seven years ago, she considered herself a Catholic and was now outraged that the yearbook—her yearbook—contained this offensive material about the Catholic mass. She pointed out that the other religious organizations were treated in a respectful and straightforward manner, and she was indignant that her religion alone was singled out for this ridicule.

As I explained that this was my first knowledge of this

incident and that I shared her outrage, I had to stifle the question that was also welling up inside me: "Why are you so irate about this sort of attack on a church in which you haven't participated for several years?" Hoping that I will someday get to ask my question, I agree with her now that I will make a formal complaint about the treatment of the Catholic Church in this year's yearbook.

Later I discover that the annual yearbook had just appeared the previous day, and in the next few days many Catholic students call or come by to show me the offensive section. But these are students whom I have seen at mass regularly over their four years. It is the outrage of the resolutely non-practicing Elaine that intrigues me. The only other time I ever see her is in the huge crowd at commencement, and I never get to ask her my question.

But every time I think of her anger in my office that day, I see in my mind's eye the television image of the sociologist and novelist Andrew Greeley explaining to Larry King one night on CNN how Catholicism becomes so much a part of people's imaginations that it is almost impossible for people to leave the church completely.

About a year later, another student has just spent the past hour calmly and very articulately explaining all the reasons behind his decision to abandon his Catholic faith. I have known Larry just well enough over the past three years to realize that he is an extraordinarily gifted and brilliant student. His parents had fled Lithuania as young people after World War II and have attached the greatest importance to their Catholic faith which has sustained them through all the chaos and sorrow of being refugees and exiles. Larry tells me of the admiration he has for his parents' faith, even for their wanting so badly to bequeath it as their most prized gift to their children. But Larry no longer believes.

Though I can feel his anguish at separating himself from

his parents on such a fundamental level, I can only be impressed with the honesty and rigor with which he has personally analyzed the issue of God whose existence he feels he is now compelled to reject. And from that rejection, he explains, he must abandon the church which is predicated, of course, on the existence of God. He has come to talk about his reasoning and to see what I think.

I am assuring myself that this is an honest mature rejection, far removed from the stereotypical adolescent rebellion and rejection of a parent's religious beliefs, but as our conversation continues on for another hour or two, I realize that he is really asking my permission or approval for his decision to abandon the church, and I am again stifling the question that is welling up with me: "If you have made the momentous decision to reject belief in God and abandon the church, why are you asking a Catholic priest, of all people, if what you're doing is all right?"

And again in my mind I hear Andrew Greeley explaining the long-term impact of the Catholic imagination.

After the summer break, I am puzzled to see Larry at mass every Sunday on campus and delighted, for the sake of my own curiosity at least, when he stops me one Sunday to set up a time to talk again. He is as convinced as ever in his atheism and rejection of the church's teachings, but, he explains, he is now attending mass out of respect for his heritage. To be true to his new convictions, he tells me that he does not take communion or join in any of the prayers at mass, but he recognizes that he still has some emotional need to be present and to identify with the Catholic community. Maybe, he says, it's just his childhood memories, or maybe its his Lithuanian heritage which he greatly values, or maybe it's just his friends in the Catholic community, or maybe it's just out of habit, or maybe, he laughs, his new convictions of unbelief are not so certain. "What do you think?" he asks me.

"Maybe, Larry," I say, "it's all of those things."

Maybe, I tell myself, it is that Catholic imagination which Andrew Greeley was trying to explain to Larry King.

IT'S THE MASS THAT MATTERS

It is very hard to leave the Catholic Church completely. Few people actually do, and even fewer join another religious tradition. Most of the studies I have seen on religious affiliation in America indicate that Catholics rarely take the step of joining another religion or church. What does not show up with statistical precision in most studies is *drift*. Catholics, especially students, drift in and out of their church affiliation, without making very clear lines of demarcation. "Yes, I'm a Catholic but not a very good one" usually means that a student does not attend mass regularly.

Rarely does a student mean, as Larry did, that he or she has made a decision about belief and unbelief. It may mean some uncertainty and difficulty with specific teachings of the Catholic Church, but only rarely is that the decisive factor. More to the point, for students at least, are a new group of friends, or a new boyfriend/girlfriend who is non-religious, or a weariness and sense of boredom with religion that was very much a part of their family, or anger over some incident with the clergy. On the other hand, when students explain why they are returning to the practice of their faith, most often they place their absence from regular worship in the context of a period of their life when they are equally inattentive to other commitments, including their families, studies and old friends. "Getting my life back on track" is often the way they describe their decision to resume mass attendance as part of getting back to their academic and other life commitments, all of which had drifted to the point where they were unhappy about themselves.

Ash Wednesday, though not a day of obligation, always draws the largest crowds of students at mass because receiving ashes may be the most profoundly truthful symbol of the human condition and its finitude, but also because ashes also graphically symbolize a moment of return, of putting the past behind one and of beginning again. Of course, for many of the students at mass on Ash Wednesday, there will be yet another drift away in the weeks or months ahead, but that is why Ash Wednesday will come around again the next year. Though other feasts are more central to Catholic faith, Ash Wednesday is so popular because it is the day and the symbol that knows us best, in our turning back, our drifting away, and returning yet again.

Students, whom I do not know, will call and explain, a bit sheepishly, that they have been invited to be the baptism godparent of a new niece or nephew, or the confirmation sponsor of a younger brother or sister, and they need "some kind of a letter from the priest at school." I always suggest that they come to see me, but sometimes it doesn't get that far. I explain (what they already know full well) that this would mean a letter indicating they are a practicing Catholic and that parishes are increasingly requiring this of prospective godparents and confirmation sponsors. If we are able to get beyond the anonymity of the phone call and actually sit down and talk about it, I find that non-practicing students generally agree that it is a fair request and that it would not make sense for a non-practicing Catholic to act in this capacity. It may still leave those students with the unresolved difficulty of explaining to their family why they cannot be the godparent or sponsor, but it usually prompts a good discussion that would never have otherwise taken place.

The discussion always confirms that, for both practicing and non-practicing students, regular mass attendance is the distinction. While almost no Catholic will claim to be a good

Catholic in the sense of living up to Catholic norms completely, nearly all are clear about regular mass attendance
being the criterion of being a practicing Catholic. That was, of
course, the clear line in my pre-Vatican II Catholic childhood,
and, despite all the changes over the years, it remains just as
clear in young Catholics today. Nothing else functions in
quite that clear and decisive way for most Catholics of all
ages. And I marvel at how deeply the mass is lodged in Andrew Greeley's Catholic imagination.

Most campus ministers and college chaplains I know
would not limit the criteria of an active or practicing Catholic
to regular worship, but would include a sense of personal
prayer, general acceptance of the Catholic tradition and its
teachings, and moral and ethical perspectives and attitudes
about social issues, fearing that mass attendance alone can be
an automatic or merely habitual practice rather than a personally thought-out commitment. Some might hasten to add that
they know "good Catholics" who, for one reason or another,
do not regularly attend mass. But most campus ministers
would add that, for most of the Catholic students they know,
regular mass attendance would be the primary criterion. In-
terestingly, my non-Catholic colleagues would use the same
norm for Catholics, even when they would not find it appropriate for their own congregations.

The centrality of the Sunday eucharist is further evidenced by the significant number of students who practice
only when they are able to do so in their campus communities. When asked why they do not also attend when they are
home or working in another city during summer and winter
breaks, they will almost always cite some feature of the Sunday celebration, usually sermons, which they find alienating,
in addition to the lack of the close community which they
have on campus. Almost never do they point to a structure, or
a parish or diocesan policy, or even to a church teaching

(unless they have heard something being obsessively pressed in sermons). Rather it is something missing or disappointing in the Sunday celebration itself that leads to their absence. In some measure this is the result of the high expectations they have acquired from their experience of Sunday mass on campus. In most cases they view their absence as temporary, until returning to campus or, if they have graduated and moved on, hoping to find a church that captures some of what they knew in their campus community.

Later we will look at the dilemmas of young single Catholics, out of college, and their estrangement from the church during the increasing number of years when they are still single, and its meaning for the American parish and the whole church.

COMMITMENT TO CATHOLICISM

"But they are mostly 'cafeteria type' Catholics, aren't they?" is the reaction of a pastor in the diocese who is surprised when I tell him how many students attend mass on campus. His friendly skepticism, which is proabaly valid for any Catholic congregation of any age group, is a reflection of some of his own experience but is more directly the result of the media image of college students. The pastor is right, in part at least, but in a more important sense he is simply unfamiliar with the whole mindset of young people.

He is concerned with the quality and longevity of commitments, but students today are tenacious in their reluctance to make commitments—to each other, to definite career plans, to political and social theories, and to religious beliefs. Long-term personal commitment, in general, whether to other people or to ideas, looms as a much more formidable prospect to young people now than perhaps it did some generations ago. First of all, they have lived only in a world of rapid change and wildly swinging pendulums. But more compelling is their own experience, more widespread now than a few generations ago, of the often devastating breakdown of commitments in their own families, the divorces of their parents or older brothers and sisters, as well as the accumulated impact of the throw-away society in which nothing seems to last very long.

Even when they are familiar with Catholic teachings, which is not always common, students bring this sense of non-committal wariness to their religious convictions. What can often appear to be dissension, or at least indifference, is frequently a more basic lack of knowledge. They may not actually know what the church's teachings and doctrines are because they have never heard them explained in any substantial manner, aside from some references in sermons or in the popular media. To this void in their religious education add their common psychological hesitancy about making commitments, and you have practicing Catholics who will also say of Catholic teachings, "But I'm not sure." On campus such skepticism can also forestall an argument when the hot Catholic issues of abortion or homosexuality are directed at someone who practices Catholicism. Students also live in an environment where, in matters like religion, only one's personal philosophy is considered valid, posing questions as "What do you think about abortion?" rather than "What does your church say about abortion?" "I'm not sure" is an answer that can not only preclude a nasty argument, but may accurately reflect a student's uncertainty of (1) what he or she really thinks about the morality of the issue and (2) of what the Catholic position is, aside from the fact that, in this case of abortion, it is against it.

This combination of sheer lack of knowledge and personal commitment is true of doctrines at the center of Catholic faith like the Trinity, the incarnation, or the meaning of a sacrament. When I present a detailed explanation of the mass, college students who have been attending mass all their lives find it fascinating, primarily because they are hearing it for the first time.

It would be inaccurate, in my experience, to view most students as either dissenters or people with their own highly individualistic, purely subjective versions of Catholicism, but it is equally inaccurate to suppose they have a developed intellectual understanding of their religion comparable to the level of their secular learning. They are waiting to see, in this as in most matters, what a yet largely unexperienced life is going to disclose to them.

For now, at this stage of life, they have a way of worship, familiar but not completely understood, in which they are able to pray and from which they derive their identity as Catholics. This is hardly unique to students or to young people. Being a Catholic means to them what it has probably meant for most Catholics, much more rooted in praying as Catholics have always prayed (in the mass and the other sacraments) than in propositional doctrines of belief.

To this description of factual identity, I must hasten to add that I find students are also eager to learn more about doctrines, how they came about and how they have evolved over the centuries, whenever that opportunity is offered in discussions or in a course which I teach on campus.

Recent years have seen a welcome emphasis in religious education on the more personal formation of the young person, but sometimes at the expense of preparing the mind to know and wrestle with the issues of faith and doctrine. Some of my colleagues joke that young Catholics do not reject doctrines like papal infallibility because they do not know that it exists. Clearly the lack of knowledge paves the way for the accumulation of endless misconceptions.

Why does the Catholic Church forbid Catholics to marry Jews? Why do Protestants have to convert in order to marry a Catholic? Why is the Catholic Church so opposed to labor unions? Why does the Catholic Church say that non-Catholics are going to hell? Questions like these, from practicing Catholics, reveal the need for more accurate and solid religious education.

CHURCH ISSUES

"Abortion, homosexuality, married priests and women priests" are the main topics of a fascinating paper by a student in one of my courses. She is planning on a career in journalism and had decided to research articles about the Catholic Church in a major newspaper over a three year period. As a non-Catholic, she had hoped to discover in her survey why people are Catholic, and was eager also to find out why some people become Catholic. She had come by a few weeks earlier to discuss the first draft of her paper but was frustrated because the newspaper articles did not really deal with her interest in why people are or become Catholic. I had then suggested that she interview a number of Catholic students right on campus, asking them why they are Catholic. Now the final version of her paper concludes that, while the newspaper coverage of the church focuses on the issues mentioned a moment ago, these issues did not really emerge in her interviews with Catholics.

Her conclusions place these issues in a much more realistic context. The questions about institutional change or reform in the church are widely publicized in the popular media but they are rarely a major factor in students' decisions to practice or not to practice their faith. About as many students go to mass precisely because the Catholic Church does not ordain women as there are who refrain from attending mass precisely because the church does not ordain women. Almost none, in both cases. If asked, the majority of students would no doubt be in favor of the ordination of women, but, like the whole range of such institutional issues, it does not determine their relationship to the faith community on campus. Nor would students want these issues, whatever their opinions about them, to be the main focus of a worship service. Nourishment, not debate, is their reason for worship.

"All politics is local" sums up the political wisdom of that master politician, former speaker of the House of Representatives, Tip O'Neil. "All church is local" might be the equally insightful religious wisdom. However well informed we might be about the global church and its many issues, most of us only experience the church in a local parish or in a campus community. Reactions and decisions, likes and dislikes, and affiliation issues are determined on the basis of what we know first-hand. Most campus faith communities, in my experience, are open and inviting, lively and spirited. They attract students who want to be part of such a community and most often succeed. By necessity, these campus communities are often less structured and massive than parish communities and have the added factor of significant turnover each year which, while draining, does create some inner flexibility. Men and women who serve as ministers in these communities are often people who prefer the rhythm and challenge of campus life. This mix of students and ministers, often drawing in some non-university people as well, is a unique expression of American Catholicism which, while not a model for all parishes, can serve as a kind of laboratory for the whole church of the future.

As the Jesuit sociologist John A. Coleman has shown (cf. the Introduction), the Catholic Church is quite effective in maintaining the allegiance of young people in the United

States. Many of these students are affiliated and have allegiance, but their stance toward the whole church, beyond the immediate campus experience, is best characterized as a "benefit of the doubt ecclesiology." Since the Church has been a part of their growing up, and knowing the strength that the church has provided for people whom they know, and aware of its large importance in history and today's world, they give it the benefit of the doubt, even when they say "I'm not sure." Something so significant, with its long survival record, cannot be easily discounted, nor can it be assimilated in one simple embrace. Something tentative, hesitant, and held-back usually seasons their view of the whole Roman Catholic Church in its entirety.

But that is a noteworthy and startling amount of allegiance, more than any other allegiance students would ever enter into at their time of life, in this time of history. Non-Catholic campus ministers and other campus observers who know students well are always amazed and curious about the phenomenon of the large crowds of Catholic students celebrating the eucharist. Whatever the rough edges and the unresolved or inconsistent elements, it is an uncommonly extraordinary event on an American campus.

CULTS

Each year there are a small number of students who join one of the highly aggressive religious groups which are commonly called cults. The appeal of these cults and their recruiting methods have been well documented, and each year all the chaplains alert the campus community to their presence and their methods, offering ourselves as a resource for anyone who wants more information or help. These groups follow a predictable pattern in their recruiting methods, seeking out students who are vulnerable at the moment and overpowering them with instant friendship, community and acceptance. Once in the group, such students typically cut ties with friends, former groups and even families, as they become strangely and totally immersed in their new religious group. Sometimes accurately described as destructive religious groups, these cults can create terrible pain in families who feel they are losing their son or daughter to something they cannot understand.

Most of us in various chaplaincies on campus try to provide as much educational and informational material about these groups so that students recognize the recruiting methods, while at the same time respecting first amendment rights and freedom of religion. But, in response to the aggressiveness of these cults, many schools have now instituted some safeguards against proselytizing and unwanted recruiting.

Fortunately most Catholic students, even if they do not recognize the group, have an instinctive dislike for their methods and firmly decline their invitations. Increasingly, parents, chaplains and university administrators are becoming concerned about these cults and are properly utilizing information, awareness and education as the best methods to combat their harmful influence.

4

Behavior / Morality / Sexuality

A SEXUAL REVOLUTION?

"You can't put the toothpaste back in the tube," said a professor at Berkeley, borrowing H. R. Haldeman's Watergate era metaphor to express his sense of the futility of reversing the "sexual revolution." A group of faculty and other adults in the campus parish met for an hour after mass each Sunday over coffee and donuts to discuss theological issues. The topic for the past few weeks had been the Vatican Declaration on Human Sexuality, approved by Pope Paul VI, which had reaffirmed traditional Catholic sexual ethics. Here in California, in 1976, in this group, there was a consensus that, among young people, a vast sea change was taking place in sexual behavior and ethics. But how far would it go?

Pre-marital sex and perhaps homosexuality were becoming commonly accepted, they felt, but would the generation formed by this revolution also abandon marital fidelity? And how far back into adolescence would sexual behavior become acceptable? Among fifteen year olds? thirteen year olds? Some in this group thought the lines drawn in the Vatican Declaration were unrealistic, but they all clearly wanted to draw some lines at least around marriage and around very young adolescents. Most were uncomfortable with the traditionalism of the Vatican Declaration but were equally alarmed about the "anything goes" direction of the sexual revolution.

Yet no one in the group was able to suggest what might or could be done. Many of them were parents of young children and were deeply frustrated at their inability to influence the atmosphere and trends in which these children were now growing up. They all wanted something but no one could quite say what that "something" might be.

Today in the early 1990s discussions about the sexual behavior of young people routinely assume that many of them are sexually active, but now the discussion is likely to focus on AIDS and other sexually transmitted diseases, date and acquaintance rape, and teenage pregnancy. The National Institutes of Health estimate that as many as one in five hundred college students has been exposed to the AIDS virus. Most universities are now instituting programs to deal with what is seen as an alarming rise on campus of rape, often committed by friends or acquaintances of the victim. At one prestigious university a prostitution ring was discovered among some of the women students. About half the nation's universities have either closed down or strictly limited fraternities and other social groups for alleged incidents of gang rape or other sexual crimes of violence.

It had been thought that the "pill" would usher in an era of sexual freedom for young people, but the revolution has now turned in directions which cause alarm even among those who do not espouse traditional values. Some of us are old enough to remember the days when sexuality was not so public. Some dread the return of what they remember only as repression. Many of us came of age in the midst of the revolution.

But today's college students have known only confusion in a society which is drenched with the commercial exploitation of sex, alongside dire warnings about the deadly consequences of what is called "unsafe sex." Add to this the changed perception of women as willing or available sexual partners (but not yet in the ads!), the hesitancy of parents to offer clear directions about sexual behavior, and the student competition to score sexually, and you can see something of the massive confusion facing the average eighteen year old. Put that eighteen year old in an academic institution which basically says, "We don't care how you behave sexually as long as you don't force yourself on anyone and you use a condom for safety," and now you are close to getting inside the head and hormones of a college freshman in the early 1990s.

In America of the 1990s no one is very happy about how the sexual revolution turned out. No one anticipated the appearance of AIDS or the increase in rape. Some of the earlier proponents of sexual freedom are now busy urging caution in light of the ravages of disease. Many who saw the sexual revolution as the liberation of women from traditional sexual constraints are now trying to stem the rising tide of sexual aggression toward women, while fighting the pornography and commercialization of sex which demean women. Staunch traditionalists, never happy about the whole development, feel vindicated.

College students, feeling all the sexual eagerness that young people do, are confused about roles, about limits, and about what is going on inside them.

Sexual behavior is, of course, not the only moral issue in this age group, but it is the most widely discussed and it is the one that inflicts the most pain. Even aside from the all-important health considerations, young people are deeply hurt by the kind of sexual behavior that is now common from early high school on. Sex is no longer something discovered in college but is part of every high school experience. Too much, too soon, too fast—this is obvious. But our culture does not provide much beyond constant sexual stimulation.

SEX, AFFECTION AND THE TIMES

The sexual revolution was in essence a demise of public consensus on standards of behavior. It was not the first time in human history when sexual behavior became unrestrained, but it was the first time it was so publicly justified and celebrated. The context in which behavior changed is probably as important as the behavior itself. Don't blame those at the margins of society, or hippies, or *Playboy,* or LSD in the water. If such were the case, the sexual revolution would also be at the margins. Instead, we need to see the two other catalysts that were to materialize at the same time and are interconnected to the changes in sexual standards.

Throughout human history people have risked their marriages, community standing, royal thrones, and even their lives for a few moments of sexual affection. The irony of this behavior and the consequences of being found out have provided endless plots for our enjoyment, from the classics of literature to the afternoon TV soap operas. We are fascinated by the emotional starvation that fuels the desperate search for the fleeting sexual assurance of affection and worth, and the suspense to see if the infidelity is caught. A loveless marriage, a lonely single life, a wounded ego, a desire to be thought young again—these are recurring motives for the illicit sexual encounter. We identify with many of these feelings, voyeueristically wondering if we or someone we know is getting ready for the fall.

The breakdown of marriage and family life in our time has produced millions of young people who are vulnerable to just such a moment of sexual affection and assurance. The more starved of family love and intimacy, the more desperate and earlier will be these sexual encounters. Two young people with the same emotional needs will find each other in a crowd within minutes. These may well be students who excel at chemistry or economics or computer science, but their emotional needs are of another world where academic accomplishment means little.

It is no coincidence that the inner problems of the American family and precocious sexual activity burst upon our consciousness in roughly the same era. Nor is it a coincidence that students from healthy and emotionally developed families are far less vulnerable to the sexual games played on campus.

The second important coincidental factor is the way young people increasingly deal with their inhibitions. Despite all the brash openness about sex in our society, people remain innately inhibited about this most revealing and intimate of all human experiences. Some inhibition does come from religious and ethical training, but it also seems to be a universal component of the human psyche. To fully participate in the sexual carnival, most young people need to lower their inhibitions, as well as providing their potential partner with a similar way to lessen his or her inhibitions. Their solution to inhibitions is the age-old and traditional one: alcohol and other drugs. Students, on this quest, do not go to parties to meet people and get drunk; they go to parties to meet a sexual partner and to drink enough together so they can wind up in bed together. The aftermath is not always so much fun.

I have never heard a student talk about a disturbing sexual encounter that did not involve the use of alcohol or some other drug. The mystery of today's phenomenon of early teenage drinking and other drug use is less mysterious when we consider the inhibitions from which teenagers want to be delivered.

The popular image of sexually robust college students usually neglects two other types of students whom you will also meet on any campus. The first is the student, perhaps a growing type, who has absolutely no moral or ethical concerns in the area of sexual behavior. Such students view the traditional restraints as something literally from ancient times, much the way most people would view proponents of a flat earth. They have simply never been exposed to such concerns in their families and schools or among their friends. They are genuinely puzzled that some people seem to have such concerns. For them sexual gratification is there for the taking whenever possible. They will often approach other moral issues, like cheating, in a similar fashion, restrained only by the possibility of being caught. Listening to them, people frequently mistakenly label them immoral, when in fact they are more accurately described as pre-moral or amoral. They simply have no experience of any kind of personal morality.

While there are young people who are innocent of personal morality, it is also apparent that this end result of the secular society is at least partially present in a much wider spectrum of people. As moral and religious norms have been increasingly relegated to the purely private sphere, many are now coming into young adulthood without personal moral norms unless they were part of the private, family or school atmosphere of their growing up.

The second group would, understandably, never attract much media attention. They subscribe to the traditional norms about sexual behavior which, as with all in moral allegiances, does not mean they always live up to them. But they do believe that sex is properly the love between a married couple, that promiscuity is degrading and wrong, and that they should struggle to discipline their sexual instincts. They are unhappy, even repentant about their lapses. They are scornful of the exploitation of sex in our commercial culture. They have respect and high regard for those who evidence sexual virtue. They often tell me that they think most students are like them, no less so for failing to attain sheer virtue.

"Just war stories" is the way they evaluate the incessant talk about sexual conquest, meaning there is often a lot more braggadocio than deeds. There is a large measure of unreality and fantasy in the youth culture's sexual universe as can be easily deduced from a casual glance at the popular films and music videos which cater to that fantasy. All of this creates pressure to be perceived as more sexually active than in fact most people are.

But college students who hold to the traditional norms are also greatly influenced by the secular, amoral treatment of sex around them. It is not clear or obvious to them which values they subscribe to at any given time. Regret, excitement, fear, shame and challenge all mix in a very confusing cauldron for most, constantly changing because of a new relationship or the last break-up.

MORAL THINKING

Moralizing alone accomplishes little, not because of the deficiency of morality itself, but because so many students are, in varying degrees, pre-moral or amoral. The practical case for moral behavior in sexuality, as in many other areas of personal life, needs to be made more persuasively. That practical case can be made, especially when it speaks to experiences they already have: promiscuity is degrading as well as dangerous, fidelity in marriage is better for everyone concerned, pornography exploits women, and sexual desire can be disciplined.

The credibility of traditional Catholic sexual ethics suffers most from its disembodied rhetoric which portrays it as only a supernatural good while its practical and valuable aspects are neglected. As with all enduring ethical norms, these have emerged from the experience of human beings, over the centuries, who have found that violations of these norms bring harm and unhappiness to themselves and disruption to their community. Morality needs to address changing times and new dilemmas, but the core human experience endures. People instinctively know this to be true, but must brace themselves against the fashionable notion that human experience has been reinvented in our time. Plausible and persuasive arguments for traditional ethics need to explore how other communities of people have wrestled with infidelity, sexual anarchy, exploitation and the dichotomy between words and actions.

"The failure of a person to live up to an ideal does not invalidate the ideal," argues John Silber, the controversial president of Boston University, in what should be his least controversial insight. In fact, he is drawing on the very Catholic tradition that the worthiness of the priest does not determine the validity of the sacrament. In the age of ubiquitous public opinion polls and surveys on every conceivable issue, we are flooded with raw data about what people do, without finding out what they think, if anything, about what they are doing. If all the best sellers on guilt and shame, and all the millions of expensive hours of therapy, are any indication, people are everywhere struggling with the discrepancy between what they think and what they do, as people have always done. Forming young people to think morally requires that we be much more ambitious than merely looking at what people do. Morality is a systematic reflection on that behavior, on one's own behavior, in light of principles and norms which are wise and have stood the test of time and human experience. Initiating young people into such reflection about themselves, their peers and their society is an extraordinary gift from a teacher, a parent or a campus minister. Moral reflection on sexuality, commitment, fidelity, and all these other highly personal issues is at least as urgent as the moral perspectives that are issued endlessly from every imaginable source on other issues.

And strangely, it is the ubiquity of moral rhetoric, not its absence, that creates a serious obstacle. If everything is moral, then nothing is moral. Even the most trivial and inconsequential issues are often spoken of with either moral passion or moral outrage. The letters to the editor in campus newspapers will have the word "moral" at least once in nearly every four sentences. The result, unfortunately, is the trivialization of morality, producing yet another yawn of indifference. In an effort to lessen the hurt of ridicule based on predjudice, one large state university last year surpassed all others in ludicrous pseudo-morality by issuing a ban on all "inappropriately directed laughter." Moral rhetoric needs to be carefully conserved for those issues which are of serious human consequences and about which people have freedom to act.

"None of these things ever happen at 2:30 in the afternoon. They always happen at 2 A.M." A campus police officer has dropped by my office with some papers for his forthcoming wedding, but we end up talking about a rash of incidents on campus involving some racial fights and an alleged rape. "If there were no booze on this campus," he says, "you wouldn't need a police force." He is making the point that nearly all these well publicized incidents happen at parties, or right after a party breaks up, when students have been drinking. Whatever the racial or sexual content of the incident, the clouded minds of the participants are a primary cause. Not an excuse, a cause. Until we deal with the pandemic abuse of alcohol or other drugs, we will not be able to get a handle on the more dangerous and self-destructive problems on campus.

SOCIAL ISSUES

United States involvement in Central America, divestment from companies doing business in South Africa, destruction of rain forests in Brazil—these are the kinds of issues which are usually given a high moral profile on campus. While the political activism of the 1960s may seem to have diminished on campus, it remains essentially true that it is larger, global, structural issues which attract the attention and action of students. Pundits and commentators today talk about the apathy of the majority of students who do not get involved in these larger causes. My own experience on campus, both in the now fabled 1960s and today, is that the majority of students, far from being apathetic, are deeply skeptical about the strategies of the activists, while often agreeing with the cause or issue. The apparent apathy does not mean that they are indifferent to the victims of apartheid or unconcerned about the rain forests, but they simply do not subscribe to the ideological strategies which are often loudly championed by a minority on campus. They see these strategies as impractical and ineffective because they do not ring true to their own experience.

Especially among Catholic students, I detect a very deep skepticism about ideological analysis. By a process akin to osmosis, Catholics seem to imbibe the precept that you cannot change larger societal problems until and unless individuals change. It is the endurance of the classical sense of virtue, the habit and action of an individual, and a sense of the requirement of personal conversion. All the laws and regulations against racism or exploitation, runs this deeply Catholic view, may well have merit, but society will not really change until people change. While this conviction is clearly embedded in contemporary papal and other church teachings on social issues, young Catholics assimilate this in an elemental and symbolic fashion through worship and their families, and above all by the validation of their own experience.

But on campuses, those who set the trendy public moral agenda usually dismiss such an approach as too individualistic, or as a denial of the corporate and structural nature of social evil. For Catholics, while there is a sense of social sin, it is only the accumulation of individual acts which creates the social sin. The concept of social or corporate evil, not derived from individual actions, remains an empty abstraction. Active, practicing Catholics are socially involved, but more likely as a volunteer helping a child or organizing a Valentine's Day visit to a nursing home, rather than as the more fashionable activists would have it. Tutoring one child or visiting an elderly nursing home resident will have greater claim and truth for these students than all the analysis about schools and nursing homes.

The sense of individual responsibility does make Catholics less sympathetic to the so-called causes of crime and more insistent that people be held accountable for their actions. With the immigrant experience usually still part of their families, they have that distinctive affection for the United States and its institutions, sometimes called patriotism, which always forms part of the gratitude inherited by the children of immigrants. Knowing how their grandparents or parents worked so hard to make a good life in the new country, they value that journey, and they expect it of others. Although these elements are somewhat indefinable and elusive, they inhere very deeply in the Catholic ethos, part religion, part politics, and part personal pride. Indeed, they inhere so deeply that most Catholics part company with what is usually heralded as social activism on campus. They simply do not buy the political analysis that undergirds the activism.

One consequence is that Catholics are generally labeled conservative (meaning unsympathetic to social problems), yet studies of the voting patterns of all Catholics show them to be quite liberal on social issues like caring for the poor and disenfranchised, but more conservative when that care seems to diminish personal responsibility.

Catholic students are supportive of church efforts in the social area, especially efforts of Catholic Relief Services or Catholic Charities, but will not be patient with purely political appeals and will be supremely impatient with any indication of collapsing religious faith into political action. There is more to religion than good works which, while absolutely essential to Christianity, are not the full story and most emphatically are not to be confused with grace.

Students have not read the papal encyclicals on social justice and are only vaguely aware of their import, but when you put aside the unhelpful labels of liberal and conservative, you find that they embody those principles in an almost instinctual manner.

Listen carefully as young Catholics discuss social problems, and you may well conclude that the teaching of Catholic social doctrine is the most successful area of all the church's efforts in moral and religious education.

At some remove from the immediate moral decisions facing students, contemporary moral philosophers and theologians debate and analyze the larger landscape of our culture against which we all make our moral choices. Increasingly, a number of these thinkers, like Alasdair MacIntyre, Stanley Haweraus and James Burtchell, are retrieving the moral framework which has guided the Christian tradition, and from its wisdom they address contemporary moral issues. Part of their enterprise involves, by necessity, critical diagnosis of how the current state of moral anarchy evolved. The strongly subjectivist and relativist manner of contemporary moral thinking is one source of confusion. College students, for the most part, are not reading moral thinkers, but the influence of subjectivism and relativism is nonetheless pervasive, even in the very language they use. "Do what's right for you." "It depends on how you *feel* about it." "I can't tell you what is right for you."

The primary casualties of subjectivism and relativism in our time have been the centrality of the common good, confidence in reasoning, rootedness in an objective order of truth, and the claims of responsibility and accountability. One could plausibly argue that these issues constitute the operative dividing lines in our culture and shed more light on the current culture wars than labels like conservative and liberal. In our culture, one movement describes most human experience as morally undifferentiated in and of itself. Moral thinking, in this mode, then becomes the process of give and take by which people name and assign moral value to their experience, based on their own view of reality, producing the popular epigram that "something may be bad for me, but fine for you."

The other movement, which is focused not only on the present but seeks the wisdom of the enduring tradition, engages in a search to know what is right, independent and transcendent of the person's experience, though attentive to that experience.

Issues like euthanasia, abortion, fetal research, and mandated sterilization demonstrate the chasm between the two movements. In the absence of an operating concept of the common good and the equally marked absence of an agreed upon objective order (or even the language to talk about it), our society resorts continually and by default to processing its claims and differences through the only arenas available— the court system.

This digression into moral thinking is by way of sketching the moral terrain on which college students find themselves, often uncomprehending and inadequately informed.

The philosophical anarchy, even more directly than the attendant behavior, produces a climate that renders most young people morally underdeveloped. Or, as the catechism would have put it, in large areas of their moral lives they have not yet reached the age of reason, a valuable marker which has little to do with physical age but everything to do with the capacity to think about moral choice and to act in freedom with personal responsibility.

On the plane of everyday reality, the confusion and anarchy manifests itself in the ignorance of the law of cause and effect. "Do this, and that will most likely happen" may have about it the aura of common sense, but we cannot understand the world of college students unless we realize that they simply do not believe in such a law of cause and effect. There is perhaps something uniquely American about this dismissal in a society that is fond of reinventing itself. Things happen; coincidences and chance abound; it's whom you know; being at the right place at the right time—but not an order of inter-related realities which, by virtue of cause and effect, have a claim on our conscience and moral decision making.

GOD AGAIN

"If there is no God, everything is permitted," worried the Russian prophet Fydor Dostoevsky, precisely describing the outcome of the secularist enterprise which has sway over elements of the whole society, but enjoys its fullest jurisdiction on the American campus. Everything is permitted, not simply because the legal constraints have fallen, but because we have internalized the legal license within ourselves as an ersatz moral compass.

Dostoevsky bonds God and our behavior, rejecting the distinction between transcendent religion and social action, making the connection which creates morality. Authentic religious faith is neither activism alone nor worship alone, it is the integration of the two in a person who lives in a way that demonstrates that God matters. Moralizing is deficient and ineffective because it primarily addresses my behavior, when my behavior is rooted in my belief or unbelief about God and my response to him. Moralizing, however valuable the issue it speaks to, cannot change people. It is a sterile and argumentative strategy which displays little confidence in the power of God's relationship to transform and redeem the human person.

On campus, as throughout the church, the call to worship God is the call to moral truth. Ministry on campus begins and ends with the worshiping community where we become a new person.

And then our task, as Luther said, is "to let God be God."

5

Parents and Family

A CRISIS

It was on my walks around Berkeley, during the Christmas-New Year's season of my first year in California, that I first began to meet students who did not want to go home for Christmas. I had always known international students who stayed around campus because the trip home was too expensive for just a few weeks. But these were students from California, just a few hours from home. I would meet a few every day that Christmas season on the deserted campus, in a bookstore or just walking. Some had gone home for Christmas Day itself and come back as soon as possible, but some had never left the campus.

"My family is such a hassle. It gets very complicated," Alex was explaining to me. "Both my parents have remarried a couple of times now. So I have a bunch of step-parents and brothers and sisters from all these marriages. If I go home I have to see all of them, and if I stay with one, the others get mad. Besides, I don't really like some of them. So it's really easier for me to stay away."

Twenty years later, on another campus at the other edge of the country, there are more students now for whom going home is a hassle—maybe not as difficult as it was for Alex, but a hassle. The intricate configurations of many families, the ill will between the former partners but still parents, and the other dislocations of American family life have left many young people without the mythic home which is always there for you. Effectively, many of the children of these families have been on their own emotionally, if not physically, since early childhood.

Countless studies now show the effects of this family crisis on everything from crime to malnutrition to critical psychological problems. We need not be surprised. The conventional family support system is now only providing its nurturing and emotional benefits for about half the students in college today.

Everyone is affected, whatever their own family situation, because the reverberations do not limit themselves to the children of a family but have impact throughout the whole society. America is relearning that the family is indispensable and irreplaceable in the social fabric of our lives. This is not the place to look for remedies to such a massive problem, but rather it is essential to know that students today often arrive on campus with vastly different emotional histories and support systems.

PARENTS DO MATTER

Parents, whether divorced, still married, or married again, need to know how important they are to their college-age daughters and sons. The glibness and nonchalance of a college student can easily lead parents to think that their usefulness and influence are over. But they should know that when they open up to other people, and of course when parents are not around, college students attach the deepest emotional and personal significance to their relationships with parents. Good, bad, or just mediocre, parental relationships grow deeper or hurt more as the years go on. You can see it in their faces when they talk about parents coming to visit, a look of eagerness or a measure of pained resignation. All students pretend they are beyond all that, as most of us do when we're determined to be newly autonomous, but it is always there. The parental relationship has no other corollary. It controls, haunts, affirms, blames, comforts, demands, nourishes and is omnipresent. Some of us who are much older, and whose parents are now dead, still find ourselves talking to them in our imaginations, discovering within ourselves a relationship that does not pass away.

The dynamics of reaching adulthood require severing the knot that binds a young person to parents in a relationship of dependency. The first years at college afford a wealth of symbolic opportunities for cutting that knot. Depending on the prior relationship, the cutting can be rebellious and edged with rejection, or sullen and silent, or merely transitional and quite natural. But it always hurts. Parents cannot help but feel shunted aside, or useless, as their children struggle to assert their own independence. Parents who do handle it well, either from experience or from common sense, just seem to take a deep breath and hold on for the duration, avoiding the common over-reactions that can scar the relationship. But some parents seem to fight it at every step, nervously holding on to some control. These are the parents who feel compelled to express strong opinions about every new boyfriend or girlfriend, about the academic major or career choices their children must make, about the way they dress, and, if they are religious, about the religious practice of their children. It makes a difference when the student is the first child or the last child, whether the marriage is undergoing inner stress, and whether the parents have new personal problems of their own. Transition is too mild a word to describe this necessary parting of the ways, as a young person becomes an adult, but it must happen, and parents, in most cases, discover they need more patience now than they did when diapers and 2 A.M. feedings were the annoyance.

The second stage of this transition is the relinking or redefining of the parental relationship. When young people do establish some sense of autonomy, of being their own person, they begin to make attempts to reconnect, but now on a very different basis. Here the most savvy and alert parents are ready to put aside the old control mechanisms and to get to know their children all over again. Equality, mutual enjoyment, even more communication and honesty can begin now to emerge in the relationship. Something akin to friendship begins to happen between some parents and their children.

But it is not effortless or routine. The new autonomy of the child gives parents the inevitable message that they are getting old, as the role of being the parent recedes. Even parents who manage it well can feel terribly frustrated when they know that, from their own experience, they could save the child from unnecessary mistakes and wrong turns. Above all else, parents need to know how to wait for the right moment, usually until the issue surfaces within the child, and then to be there for the young person's support and friendship. Here, as in football, stand-up comedy or world affairs, timing is everything.

PARENTS ARE THE LAST TO KNOW?

After a chaplains' panel discussion on student life which is held on Parents' Weekend, the parents of a junior student came over and introduced themselves. As soon as they gave me their names, I knew whose parents they were. I was then utterly confused when they quickly explained that I would not know their daughter since she had dropped her religious practice ever since arriving at college. But, in fact, I knew their daughter well and saw her at mass every Sunday. I held my tongue as I tried to fathom why she had obviously been giving her parents a very different message. Her parents and I chatted for a while, but my mind was full of questions: Why would she want her parents to think she had given up her religion? Should I ask the daughter about this? Were these parents the only ones who didn't know she practiced her religion? Was she punishing her parents for something?

Some years before the mother of a student who tragically committed suicide had said to me, "Parents are the last to know." This parent had just listened to her son's friends speak at an interfaith memorial service held on campus some weeks after his death. His friends had all made some reference to the problems her son had been having for a number of years, and after the service his mother tells me that she and her husband never realized how serious his problems were. Her words to me that afternoon, "Parents are the last to know," describe the deepest fear of many parents I have talked with. The slightest evasion in response to a question can trigger it, or a change in attitude, or a new set of friends, or the outright but obvious falsehood. Parents can easily imagine the worst, especially when they are miles or hours away. Waiting for the right moment to talk about it can seem as if it is only adding to the fear of the unknown. Perhaps more helpful would be a recognition of the mistakes parents commonly make when gripped with such fear. The first mistake always involves the telephone, calling roommates, friends, administrators, or a chaplain, in an effort to find out what is really going on. A student somehow always finds out about these telephone calls and will feel spied on. Whatever trust remains will be damaged.

These phone calls also have the potential to damage a whole set of relationships between possibly troubled students and friends or advisors on campus. I have found this to be so true that, when a parent calls me to find out what's wrong with a son or daughter and adds, "Don't tell that I called," I quickly explain to parents that I cannot continue to talk with them unless they understand that I must tell the son or daughter that the parent has called me.

The other common mistake is the explosive angry confrontation which frequently drives the problem deeper into hiding. Students tell me of threats to cut off tuition, expense money or some other support. In too many situations I have seen this course of action lead both parents and children down a path of estrangement from which return is unlikely.

In fact, parents are rarely "the last to know." They may not yet know all the details of what they are sensing in their son or daughter, but most parents have a sixth sense about their own children and, if they are not in a complete state of denial, will be among the first to know that something is not right. But they need to understand that this is a potentially volatile point in their relationship. It's time to rely on the old bromides because they are the best available: patience, calm, reason, and trust that a better moment will arrive. Parents who handle this difficult moment well typically look to each other for support and emotional assurance rather than frantically seeking it in an explosive confrontation with their son or daughter.

THE DYSFUNCTIONAL FAMILY

Shortly after our primitive ancestors began to emerge from their cave dwellings, they discovered or invented the family as the best method of raising children and contributing to the common welfare of the whole tribe. As attested from the earliest records we can garner, all religions accordingly put the family at the apex of the values to be honored and protected. Now after the cultural maelstrom that has battered the family in our culture, we are in the position of reinventing the wheel, of discovering, as if for the first time, what our primitive ancestors discovered about the family and its role in making us who we are.

One of the most visible signs of this rediscovery is an avalanche of books, TV talk shows and new jargon about what has become known as *the dysfunctional family.* Like other things in our Geraldo Rivera-Phil Donahue-Oprah Winfrey culture, it is being grossly overdone, applied to everything from our sex lives to our crime rates, and producing its new set of excuses for our own selfish and mindless behaviors. Many of us, especially with some religious perspective, reject its inherent determinism, not in the least because we all know people from very troubled families who bit the proverbial bullet and, not pausing too long in the swamp of self-pity, went on to make good lives for themselves. Maybe we did ourselves.

Yet it is still worth our attention because the concept of *the dysfunctional family* has obviously struck deep resonating chords in our society. However new the jargon, it represents a perennial wisdom about the effect of family life for good or for ill on children. Families are now being called dysfunctional because of the behavior of a member, usually a parent, who has a lasting effect on the lives of the children, including the observable tendency of such children to repeat the destructive behavior of the parent. Child abuse, alcohol and drug addiction, mental illness and socio-economic factors are among the most prevalent problems in the dysfunctional family syndrome. Some truths seem inescapable about these families. First, denial of the problem is frequently the common response of the children and other family members. Second, victims of child abuse often become themselves the abusers of children, as the children of addicted parents often become addicted in time themselves.

The effect of the talk shows and the self-help books is that the concept and the language of the dysfunctional family is accessible to everyone as people try to understand their own family backgrounds. College students, even those who don't watch Oprah (but so many of them do!), will hear a great deal of it in their courses in the social sciences. Naturally such a pervasive concern leads almost all of us to look at our family and its role in our own development. Very real problems, increasingly coming to light, like child abuse and addiction, must be dealt with, optimally by a whole family together but at least by each member who is able to pierce the barrier of denial.

A student drops by to ask me to pray for his forty-four year old father who is having very serious health problems brought on by diabetes and high blood pressure. He tells me that it would be best if his father gave up drinking because it obviously has led to some of these health problems, but he assures me, and himself, very vehemently that his father is not an alcoholic because he has always been employed. This son already has a reputation among his own peers for being a big drinker on campus.

Another student, whose parents have been divorced for many years, tells me of the family intervention she initiated about her mother's drinking. The hardest part, she tells me, was getting her brothers and one sister who live a thousand miles away to take part in the intervention. For a long time they did not want to acknowledge that there was a problem, telling this sister, "Mom only drinks too much on holidays." Well, this student says, "the only time they ever see her is on holidays." She consulted with a trained alcohol counselor and planned an effective intervention which led to her mother seeking treatment. Now after a year and a half of sobriety, she tells me she has gotten her mother back and she has come to a more peaceful understanding of the effect it has had on her. In this case, denial was finally shattered and life was renewed.

These two students suggest different patterns of handling family problems. One leads to repetition fueled by denial. The other uses the smarts and experience of people who have been through it and produces healing and growth. None of us should spend the rest of our lives bemoaning the fate that our families bequeathed to us. But there are formidable problems. There are also tools and methods of dealing with these problems so that they do not continue to define and limit us. Parents, students, counselors, chaplains and friends can educate themselves to be such tools and, when possible, to be part of a better solution.

Students who have been deprived of family support will find it somewhere else. One solution on campus is the gang— not the street gangs of recent films, but a tight, cohesive group with inner dynamics like the street gangs, though without the guns. The group becomes all-important, essential and controlling because it appears to satisfy the emotional needs which the family could not. Such students have little identity aside from the group. Their thinking, behavior, tastes and even the way they dress will be group-determined. Once formed, the group isolates itself from outsiders or other influences. Its members can easily spend four or five years on campus virtually enclosed within the group, unknown and unaffected by others. The normal developmental stages get postponed until the group moves on or falls apart, producing a painful crisis for its members.

Other students seek a surrogate for the parent who was not really a parent. Some find a mentor, an older person who provides assurance, trust, and some direction, partially filling the void of the absent or missing parent. Others enter into a disciple-like, dependent relationship with an older person which diminishes or precludes the autonomy the young person will need to acquire. The difference is in how surrogates function, how perceptive they are to the needs of students, and how clear headed surrogates are about their own emotional needs. These relationships are common and can be immensely beneficial or yet another extension of the dysfunctional syndrome. Teachers, coaches, counselors, chaplains and even older students need to be aware of what is being asked of them by students and how the dynamics of the missing parent function in these relationships. With an increasing number of students with such needs, all of us who serve in adult roles on campus require greater skill and understanding in helping students for whom the missing or absent parent is an unresolved need.

FAMILY REALITY

"Happy families are all alike; every unhappy family is unhappy in its own way," wrote Leo Tolstoy a century ago in his classic novel *Anna Karenina*. Long before the contemporary crisis of the American family, he warns us about the impossibility of generalizations about family problems. We need to be attentive to the family stories of the students, if they're up to telling them, and to avoid inserting them into pre-set categories. Each story is unique not only in its details but most clearly in experience of each member of that family. Especially when there have been serious problems, a young person will feel that nothing quite like this has ever happened to any other family before. This sense of uniqueness makes young people rigidly closed and protective about their family problems. "No one must ever know what happened in my house." Unless they find a safe place and a trusted listener, they will bury their "secrets" so deep that it will distort their lives for years to come. Simple, inquiring and non-threatening questions about family can often bring out the story which in the telling alone brings relief and healing.

Without pigeonholing families into categories, we all need a better view of what American family life is factually all about. At least two out of every five young people today are from divorced families. If we keep using standard references to the traditional family, about half of our congregation will feel left out. About half of the student congregation will have at least two homes, possibly two families, to visit or share a holiday with. A large part of that number will have grown up moving back and forth on some custodial schedule between two parents. Complicated arrangements with grandparents and step-parents are common. In a *New York Times* article (July 23, 1991), Jane E. Brody surveys some of the recent research on the effects of divorce. Twenty-three percent of divorced fathers had had no contact with their children in the past five years, while another twenty percent had not seen their children in the preceding year, meaning that, for nearly half of the children of divorce, the father is virtually absent. Ms. Brody cites the research of a California psychologist, Dr. Judith S. Wallerstein, who has studied divorced families and their children since 1971, about the effects of no-fault divorce. "Divorce on demand has turned out to be a disaster for children" because this less difficult way out for the parents has only made more widespread the inability of parents to shield their children from the harm of divorce. Ms. Brody summarizes the available research: "The commonness of divorce—half of marriages contracted in the 1970s will not last—may have reduced societal scorn and parental shame, but shows no signs of alleviating the anguish of the children." What the research cannot yet know, of course, is the effect of all this on marriages of the children, their readiness and expectations for commitment and the future of what we are relearning to be the basic and irreplaceable fabric of our lives. Nor can the research show us the solution, except perhaps to lead to what we already know.

If you are from one of those happy families which Tolstoy says are all alike, be grateful but generous. Do not assume your friends, or your children's friends, have similar experiences. If you are from a family that has had its own unhappiness, do not let the uniqueness of that sadness isolate you from the experiences and resources of others who have been through family problems. You do not have to limit yourself to what has been. There is more.

CATHOLIC WISDOM

Leo is almost a stereotype of the Irish Catholic. Outgoing and personable, very sports minded, endowed with good brains but a B student, he never misses Sunday mass. He came by to introduce himself to the priest on campus during his first week as a freshman, telling me all about his parish back home and that he often thinks about becoming a priest himself. But now over lunch one day, he is almost belligerently demanding that I assure him the Catholic Church will never change its teaching about the permanence of marriage, or as he is putting it heatedly, "the church should never screw around with divorce." Leo's parents divorced when he was twelve and the divorce is the controlling metaphor of his life through which he views all reality. "Divorce really sucks" is his occasional theological aside as he describes his father, about whom he is unforgiving. After twenty years of marriage and four children, Leo's father, a very successful attorney, informed his wife and then his children that he was seeking a divorce so that he could marry another woman. Leo explains that she was a much younger woman, a law clerk still finishing law school, and that his father's affair with her lasted all of one year. Some years later his father did marry another woman, but his mother has never remarried. Leo has told me before of the contempt he has for a Catholic high school religion teacher, a priest, who spent half (Leo's estimate?) of the senior year marriage course urging sympathy and understanding for people who divorce. Leo is certain that this priest has no divorces in his family because no one who knew divorce first hand would ever be so tolerant of such a thing. In high school, some of his teachers were alarmed at his levels of anger, and, at their suggestion, his mother got him to go for counseling. But, as Leo tells it, "the shrink tried to get me to see things from my father's point of view." Leo is still angry, and I get along with him very well because I have been either smart enough or cowardly enough not to suggest that he look at things from his father's viewpoint.

Listening to Leo's demands about the Catholic Church and divorce, I am relieved that he is a college student and not someone in charge of any pastoral ministry, but I do find the angry clarity of his sense of right and wrong refreshing. And he has a point. I have heard other students from divorced families, in less vociferous ways, talk the same way. No one is more opposed to divorce than the children of divorce, except perhaps for divorced people themselves. After all the usual words about "it's better for the children than an unhappy marriage" or "the marriage was dead anyway," we must be clear in our ministry and teaching that divorce and its ensuing family break-up cause great pain and hurt, and that people undertaking marriage need to think through the wondrous and awesome responsibility of family life. And we might well add, as an acknowledgement to Leo's pain and righteous anger, that people need to think twice before throwing it all away for, as Leo puts it, "a few tosses in the sack."

College campuses are peopled with the children of divorce and they hurt because of it. A society which has now accepted and streamlined divorce has not understood the full consequences. But any group of college students would have plenty to tell you.

A SILENT KIND OF LOVE

About family love, the poet T.S. Eliot writes, "There's no vocabulary . . . all other love finds speech. This love is silent" (*The Elder Statesman*). The love within the family is quiet and silent, requiring little by way of declaration, because it is a given, a constant, something always waiting, something you can always return to. Almost unseen, hardly noticed, it feeds us, clothes us, providing us with a security far deeper than all our later accomplishments and successes. In today's jargon, it is the bedrock of our self-esteem, the place where we discovered that we were acceptable and lovable before we even knew such words. Its absence or diminishment can only make us more acutely aware of how, like oxygen, we must have it. For the church and our ministries on campus, the crisis of American family life must be a constant awareness, not because we hold some quick fix or ready answer, but because, knowing this "silent love," we realize the toll it can take when it is not there. And for many students now it has not been there. We can never make up for that loss, but we can be part of the healing that brings a wholeness even to this wound. We can learn enough to be able to communicate at least that we know and that we are there for the duration, especially for those who, until now, have felt that no one is really there for very long. Without harshness or judgment, we can speak truthfully about commitments and how we all depend on them for life, how we know the pain their lapses and violations cause, that our failures, and the failures of parents and families, need not be a last word. And in a world of shattered commitments and broken promises, we might be people who mean what they say, whose word is good and who stay on for the duration. Young people are looking for the God who, having once said "yes," does not retract or abridge that "yes." And, in the communities of faith where we gather, God's faithful "yes" finds attentive ears.

6

Growth and Decision

"How do couples like us deal with raising their children? How do they resolve their religious differences? Do you know couples that have been able to do it well?"

Susan has been peppering me with questions like this which obviously stem from her long relationship with another graduating senior, Michael, who is from a very different family background than hers. As we talk, I am learning that Susan has two different personalities which might be disturbing, except in her case both personalities are very impressive. The Susan I have known until this afternoon is an extremely outgoing, vivacious, fun-loving and popular student. She has been going out with Michael now for about two years, and graduation, just two months away, is causing her to wonder about the future of their relationship. The Susan I have mostly known is a very secure woman whose family is very close, and is the center of much of her life. She is going on to law school after graduation to begin a career which she clearly plans to combine with marriage and children. Her religion is very important to her in a direct, matter-of-fact way that derives from her family experience.

Michael is very different. Both of his parents are divorced and remarried, and he is largely alienated from his father. He was brought up with no religious background, and all religion is very much an obscure and unattractive realm for him. He and Susan have talked a great deal about their views on marriage. He also looks forward to being married, but is much less interested in having children. While he assures her that he would never disparage her religious practice, he does tell her that he believes strongly that, if there were children, they should not receive what he calls "religious indoctrination." Susan tells me she senses that he is skeptical about her family and prefers to believe that close family life is stifling. The closeness of graduation and likely geographical separation has led to many intense discussions of the future of their relationship and the differences in their views of marriage.

This afternoon the thrust of Susan's questions and concerns surprises me. Like most who know Susan and Michael, I have always seen them as two people who really fit together, who are right for each other. But I am more surprised at the other Susan who has been emerging in our conversation this afternoon. This Susan is a person who really looks to long-range consequences and who is eager to learn from the experiences of others. This Susan is quite convinced about the seriousness of the differences between her and Michael and does not allow her obvious affection for Michael to dull her perception of their importance. She is now on the verge of an important decision which, for her, is grounded in her steady conviction that her future will be the product of her decisions in this, as in other less emotional issues. As we end our conversation, she tells me that she realizes she has a very important decision to make.

The Susan who emerged in this conversation surprised me greatly because, for all her stereotypical college student demeanor, Susan is not a product of the American youth culture. As they say, she is coming from somewhere else.

The American youth culture, already becoming a planetary phenomenon, has generated a powerful and engrossing matrix from which young people must struggle into adulthood. Freedom, spontaneity, a distinctive spoken dialect and a universal music idiom make this youth culture immensely inviting and alluring, not only to American youth but to their peers throughout the world. It casts its seductive spell even on those who are much older, inciting them to indulge themselves in a fantasy of never-ending youthfulness, while also providing a key to understanding the young products of its pervasive influence. With its films, music groups and their recordings, its clothing and insignia, it may well be the most successful economic enterprise of our time.

The global appeal of this youth culture rests on its dazzling multi-media assertion of liberation from cultural and personal inhibitions, as well as freedom from the artistic and conventional restraints of the past. For most young people, this freedom is markedly more personal than political, though clearly, as was seen in central and eastern Europe, the symbols of this youth culture have been readily grafted onto contemporary political movements for freedom.

At the core of this culture is an abiding resistance to all suggestions of cause and effect or, as some might put it, a denial of the validity of the laws of cause and effect. The icon of this culture, the MTV type music video, brilliantly captures this disdain for cause and effect by juxtaposing images without any inherent coherence, often with a dazzling display of technological proficiency. Like the culture which produces and markets them, these videos invite you to enter a world in which things do not merely happen because of prior actions, but occur because each moment or image is newly created *ex nihilo.* Context, precedent, causation and fixed meaning are swept away in a powerful fantasy, wholly subjective for each viewer, which elicits a responsive awe at the utter freedom of each moment from its past, while abruptly editing away any reference to future results. It would be difficult to find anyone, of any age group, for whom this absolute spontaneity is not a marvelously attractive beacon.

And yet it is precisely the power of these images which creates the cultural context in which young people have great difficulty navigating the journey of growth and maturity. For many who have grown up in this culture, there is no inner reference to consequences, to future outcomes predicated on present actions. There is no pattern, no law of cause and effect. Even when faced with indisputable evidence, for example the correlations of drinking, driving and lethal accidents, the youth culture prompts its adherents to claim highly personal exemptions from these consequences. "These things just happen" and "That's your problem" are common expressions of this denial of the connectedness of human choices and subsequent actions.

A few years ago, two students, close friends from their high school days, had spent a summer evening drinking which culminated in the tragic, accidental death of one of them when his friend mistakenly ran over him with his car. Weeks later, after classes had resumed, friends of the deceased asked the chaplains to conduct an inter-faith memorial service at which a number of these friends spoke. One of them used the occasion to remember fondly the good times he had shared with the deceased, not hesitating to celebrate their use of alcohol on these occasions. Two days after that memorial service, two of those who were present came to see me because they were troubled at the wild party which had ensued among these friends later on the night of the memorial service. Even here, immediately after commemorating the unnecessary death of a close friend, many of the survivors were able to exempt themselves from similar consequences.

But there were at least two who found this unreality troubling, raising the dilemma of why some students are able to opt for reality while surrounded by its denial.

MATURITY

"They don't really tell you what you need." "I really didn't know at the time I was screwing up." Frank and three of his fraternity brothers have waved me over to a table in the student union where they are whiling away a bleak January afternoon, bemoaning their fate after graduation which is only four months away. They invite me to join them by joking that things are so bad they might all become priests. Like the other seniors at their fraternity, they have been posting all their rejection notices from graduate schools and jobs, and now they suggest they might need to build an addition to hold all their "rejection wallpaper."

As I listen to them, I realize they are searching for some reasons why they have not been accepted at the law school or medical school they wanted, or why they are not being hired by business. I offer the scant consolation that the economy is very bad right now, but they are focusing on the poor grades they got in their first years, or on not taking the courses that are required by certain programs, or on how difficult it is to get good recommendations from professors when you have never spoken to them before this. Their consensus is that they should have been told all this very clearly when they were freshmen. But I can see that their present frustration is also realizing that they probably were told all this but didn't pay much attention at the time.

When students tell me about their difficulties, brought on by their own actions or, more commonly, by their inaction, my memory retrieves a definition of maturity which I often heard, with appropriate indifference, in my own youth: maturity is the capacity to postpone pleasure. And while it now leads me to bemoan my own failures to absorb the wisdom of this definition, I also realize that, at the time of first hearing this, I was not being constantly bombarded with contrary messages. However much I failed to discipline myself with sensible postponements of pleasure, the culture in which I was growing up regularly assured me that this postponement was a worthwhile achievement. People who displayed maturity were widely admired, and my own acquisition of this quality was expected, even demanded.

Contrary messages are now commonplace. "Pleasure is for now, for the moment when you feel the attraction." From the emotionally charged desires for sexual pleasure to the more routine escape of sleep, the culture urges immediate gratification. Impulse buying, whether of clothes or compact discs, is a strategy which this economic enterprise shrewdly uses, with great success, to capitalize on the youth culture's celebration of immediate pleasure.

Unless a young person is able to secure some distance from the pervading culture, growth into maturity and responsibility is increasingly difficult and most often delayed. Sometimes critical events force its development, but for the most part the American adolescent enjoys the protective environment of the youth culture until well after the college years. During this time they are able to postpone most of the demands of ordinary life which require an adult response. Intelligence and higher levels of education do not assure maturing and can typically co-exist with surprising immaturity. Colleges and universities tend to structure an exemption from ordinary life into their patterns of governance, offering students a wealth of intellectual stimulation but sheltering them from the more pedestrian demands of living in "the real world."

Student habits, in dealing with academic work or other responsibilities, are frequently marked by procrastination and a lack of future planning. Some who are obviously very intelligent are unable to get work done on time or in the required manner, thus never managing to acquire the grades and references that are necessary for further advancement. So pervasive is the pattern of postponement and procrastination that it is regularly only in senior year that students realize that the consequences of their performance may by now have eliminated many of their future career and educational options. Always there are students who have been determined from freshman year about their grades and their plans for medical school or law school or whatever, but even at excellent schools these students stand out in contrast to the dominant atmosphere. Determined students must also discover for themselves some mechanism by which they can extricate themselves from the common behavioral patterns around them. Frequently they find that they must place themselves outside the widespread social life on campus.

Social psychologists have developed schematic formulas of growth and development, based on studies and observations, which outline chronological stages in this process of maturation. The validity of much of this work can be verified by even casual contact with young people. But even this validation can be misleading when it neglects the impact of the prolonged immaturity embedded in the youth culture and hesitates to affirm the personal sense of responsibility for oneself which constitutes maturity. The confusion which surrounds the nature of maturity is not limited to the young but is frequently shared by those who study the young.

Maturity slowly begins to appear when people, of any age, embrace the reality that most, but obviously not all, of their future experiences will be the determined result of the choices and decisions, whether by action or inaction, that they have previously made. While always aware of the improbable (sudden illness, accidents, earthquakes and other future chance events), the mature person draws sensible lines of connectedness, based on personal as well as communal experience, between the present and the future. This intuitive grasp of reality is quite different from spurious and unreal future planning, which often escapes the very reality of the future by clouding it in hopeless detail. Nor is this intuitive maturity an arrogant claim to a future for which no one can claim ownership. Maturity is rather an abiding sense of consequences, even when those consequences cannot be clearly recognized, and which fills the present, its actions and choices, with a serious and reverent sense of importance. A moment's hesitancy before speaking, a decision to decline a popular social event, a serious conversation with someone before making a decision, and even a hour or two spent alone thinking are all ways in which you can detect the emergence of maturity in a student. These indications often appear as a student begins to assess the futility of how time and energy is typically consumed on campus or when the desire for a specific future outcome begins to claim as much attention as the prevailing youth culture.

Increasingly, many students do not discover clear career or professional objectives, even by the end of their college days, and they devote much of their time to frequently changing relationships, to the social life that easily becomes primary, or to some other campus activity which absorbs much of their life, encouraged in all this by a cultural impetus to live for the moment.

BREAKING THROUGH

I had come to Clemson University to give a series of talks sponsored by the Catholic chaplaincy. The talks were all at night, leaving me free during part of each day to roam the unfamiliar campus where I did not know a single student. But the flow and ebb of campus life was familiar and, after the ritual browsing of the campus bookstore, I found an empty table in

the crowded student union where I could sit, drink some coffee and observe the campus scene unfold—hundreds of students coming in and out, with books, looking for friends, engaging in the universal rituals of student life. Quickly, however, my
attention was focused on the table behind me where about six
or seven students were having what seemed to be a very intense discussion. Not so innocently eavesdropping, I could
hear them appraising the personal lives of a number of older
people on campus. From spotty references here and there, I
gathered that a few professors, a coach, and, as I later learned, a
very well known local Protestant pastor were the subjects of
this fascinating discussion.

Interspersed with some harmless gossip, I could hear a
lot of admiration for how these people lived their lives, conducted their professions, and handled their marriages and
family lives. Obviously these students were intrigued by what
they observed in the lives of these adult figures and were
busy in their conversation trying to ferret out the inner work-
ings of these impressive people.

I wondered, as I enjoyed my voyeurism, if the professors,
the coach and the pastor—all unknown to me—would ever
know that they were intriguing role models for a random
group of students in a campus cafeteria. And I concluded,
from all the colorful speculation I was overhearing, that none
of these students had ever talked directly with any of these
adults about the very things which now consumed their rapt
attention.

Students have immense curiosity about the lives of people who appear to have discovered sense, meaning and a
measure of fulfillment. But their heightened curiosity is
matched only by their youthful shyness in probing people
deeply. Frustrated by the distance they feel with admired
people, who are usually older and in some sense authority
figures, they turn to each other and, among themselves, al-

most obsessively dissect and scrutinize elders for whatever meaning they can glean from their observations. In a student union cafeteria, or on line in the campus bank, or sitting behind a group of students on a public bus, you overhear their rapid-fire conversations which frequently focus on parents, professors, other students, even campus ministers, as they try to figure them out and how they lead lives that seem to have meaning. Only their conversations about their own boyfriend/girlfriend relationships are comparable in intensity.

Since it is only the very rare student who will actually ask such people for insight, it is incumbent on those of us who work with students to take the initiative, to say something about our lives, our struggles and what we have discovered. Wisely assuming that their curiosity about our lives is not a license to lecture at them, we have a valuable opportunity to let them see how we work inside. I frequently marvel at how little students know about the personal lives of even their most available and popular professors, yet students who approach a teacher may be far more curious about how the teacher manages career and family, or how he or she deals with friends and enemies, than about the dominant theories in organic chemistry or the origins of the cold war.

Students cast their eyes around the adults they know, especially on campus, looking for opportunities to understand the adult process to which they aspire, seeking at least partial models of maturity. Their searching is indirect and far from clear in their own minds. They do not know exactly what they are looking for and would be hard pressed to frame their curiosity in precise questions. But opportunities constantly present themselves which can turn into important discussions. Adults, who wisely assume that students are on this search, can be sensitive to these signals and know how to respond, even when not directly questioned.

THE FAMILY FACTOR

A national survey reveals that the objective considered most essential by the entering freshman class of 1991 is "being well off financially" (73.7 percent). The impulse to launch into the ritual lament about the rise of materialism or consumerism among the young needs to be tempered by two considerations: (1) try to imagine any seventeen or eighteen year old of any time or culture who would not make the same determination; (2) look at what the freshman class of 1991 rates in second place as their most important objective in life—"raising a family" (67.7 percent). The turmoil of the American family notwithstanding, even the youngest students give evidence of the centrality of the family.

The family life and experience which a student brings to the college life is often the critical element in the maturing process. Some families are very successful in creating a sense of responsibility and maturity, not only by way of example, but by having the skill to demonstrate the practical validity of personal responsibility. Such families provide their sons and daughters with a counter-balance to the prevailing culture. Nevertheless, parents in these families will frequently be frustrated and even despairing when they see their efforts overwhelmed by other influences and must remind themselves, if they are realistic, that even the most successful family influence is only one of many powerful influences on young people. Yet the children of these families do have *something* to come back to, especially when they exhaust the possibilities of an experiment with a less sensible alternative. It does not soothe anxious parents to hear again that they should be patient and wait, but as they nervously watch a son or daughter veer from one experiment to another, they need to reflect on the likelihood that the environment of their sound family life will assert itself in time. And they need to muster the patience which knows that even the most basic and self-evident realities have to be discovered by each young person for himself or herself, often only after all the alternatives have been tried and found wanting. Needless to say, some of these experiments, for example with drugs or other health matters, may be so self-destructive that a skilled intervention will be more warranted than endless patience.

Parents should know that a major part of these alternative experiments will be largely rhetorical, as young people commonly adopt positions or contrive arguments to test their parents, to shock them, or as a tool in the confusing assertion of their youthful autonomy. Even students who evidence in their lives a strong commitment to their parents' values would seldom openly cite their parents as the source of such values, certainly almost never to their peers, and absolutely never to their own parents. The gratitude which successful parents receive for their efforts and sacrifices is deep and lifelong, but most will have to wait until the college years have passed before they will hear it directly from their sons and daughters.

Students from families with severe problems have often been forced into a precocious maturity which, now when they are on their own, impedes and retards their own maturity development. During their high school years some students already have assumed the role of parents, looking after younger brothers and sisters, because of the absence or impairment of one or both of the parents. Frequently students have also acted as a guardian or pseudo-parent to a parent who was unable to function normally because of the psychological aftermath of a devastating divorce, alcoholism, or other forms of psychological impairment. These are students who learned too young the skills of taking care of children, the house, shopping, cooking and even paying the bills. Now in college, especially when they have also moved away from the home, this early adulthood reverses itself in fast order, and the students who had too much maturity at so young an age now seek to recapture all that lost time, while frequently nursing a deep bitterness about their earlier fate.

Other students will explicitly reject and angrily denounce their parents' values. A group of friends, a professor, a boyfriend/girlfriend, or some emotional confrontation will influence them profoundly, at least for a time, and cause great pain to their parents. Frequently a student will also be markedly different from brothers and sisters who maintain a good relationship with their family. Sadly, many parents interpret this as a sign of their failure as parents and berate themselves—or worse, each other—for this failure. Reality may offer scant consolation, but it does indicate that even the most effective parents are only one of many influences on a young person in our society and that all influences, perhaps especially the most beneficial ones, are very fragile.

THE RELIGION FACTOR

As I have pointed out earlier, students have many reasons and ways of turning to religion. Much of it is directly related to the struggle for maturity. Some students hold fast to their religion all through college, motivated in large part by their need to have a counter-force to the prevailing culture in which they inevitably participate but about which they are also genuinely fearful. Life on an American campus often makes their need for a grounding more compelling now than earlier. I have known many students who describe their Catholicism as an anchor or a mooring in the midst of what they experience as a turbulent and chaotic milieu. This is not to say that they experience their religion primarily as an escape from this atmosphere because, in fact, they are pulled by its allure and confusion as much as anyone else. What distinguishes them from some of their peers is their hope that they will not become lost permanently in its swirl, and with at least one hand (like Sunday mass attendance) they hold on tenaciously to what they know has the capacity to survive the turmoil. There is an element of fear in their religious practice—not fear of God, but fear of themselves and their own capacity for being pulled along in a current which, for all its attractiveness, makes them profoundly uneasy.

Campus ministers who understand the cultural complexity in which their congregations live will avoid the condescension and patronizing attitude, adopted by some clergy, that this fear is simply evidence of a psychologically immature faith. While it is true that a fully developed Christian faith should motivate us to go out and change the world, there is also a long tradition that describes faith as a bulwark and shelter from threatening forces. Christian faith is, among many other things, an anchor, cast deep into stormy seas, which ties us to the permanence and transcendence of a loving God. Knowing something of the chaos of campus life, campus ministers will explore the capacity of faith to sink roots deep enough to be nourished from more enduring springs.

Always there are students who are taking a look at religion, or again at their own religion, to see if it does provide a counter-weight to the culture in which they live. Their curiosity is nearly always first piqued by a friend or a classmate who seems to be connected to a more permanent and stable personal equilibrium. The time may come, on a different schedule for everyone, when this equilibrium seems immensely desirable. If the friend or classmate appears, however obliquely, to have some religious faith and practice, the curiosity will often home in on that very mysterious element. But the curious student is in a very awkward position. "Won't my questions sound dumb?" "Do I really want to do what's involved?" "Could I really change?" "Do I want to change?"

Curious students are at mass every Sunday, watching, wondering, sometimes silently, often attempting some tentative conversation afterward. And I remind myself, in preparing the sermon for Sunday, that part of the congregation will be very much like the congregation Paul addressed, without much success, at the altar of the Unknown God.

"NOT EVERYBODY GROWS UP"

In a world that happens "on the fast track," a lot can happen in five years. It has become a marker for me in knowing students, which is why I enjoy meeting students five years (or so) after graduation. It happens frequently at the weddings of former students when many of the guests are people whom I had known in their college years, and now the conversations are full of catching up. The kid who used to wear a baseball cap, worn backward, into Sunday mass on campus is now finishing his residency in surgery. The alienated woman student who used to scold me about the bourgeois enslavement of being a parent in a traditional marriage with a conventional career is now a lawyer, married, and comparing notes on day care with another friend. The party animal, whose nineteen year old perpetually bloodshot eyes were a tribute to an enormous capacity for beer, is now in a three piece suit, without a speck of redness in his eyes, introducing his fiancée and telling me about the computer research firm of which he is the vice president. I remind myself of the wisdom in waiting for at least five years after graduation before thinking you know.

But five years later, I also meet the former student who is still talking about the things she is going to do. It is the same list she had in sophomore year. And I meet the former student who still has a tale of woes to tell, still unsuspecting what everyone else has long since concluded—that his woes are all self-inflicted. Yet another student has achieved no greater distance from her emotionally brutal father than she had in her freshman year. For some, five years represent little change and less growth. The laws of cause and effect and the discovery of personal responsibility have eluded them. And as I have learned from nearly twenty-five years of these five-year catchups, some may never grow up.

Routinely I remind myself and others that college students are young and unfinished people, but I also know how pivotal those years are on the journey of growing up. A diploma, not full-blown maturity, is conferred at graduation. To expect otherwise is foolish. But important elements of maturity are either discovered during those college years, or squandered, perhaps never to be discovered.

WHEN IT HAPPENS

The city council of the town in which the university is located was debating a zoning ordinance which embodied a negotiated compromise between the town and the university regarding new buildings, parking, traffic and other causes of conflict between our particular town and gown segments. Watching it with only half attention on the local cable access channel, I was brought to full attention when the city council opened up the meeting to comments from its citizens. A steady procession of townspeople, mostly working class men and women, poured forth to the microphone to detail the horrors of student behavior in their neighborhoods bordering on the campus. A question was raised repeatedly by the speakers and the members of the council: What can be done to get these kids to grow up?

Maturity, like other intangibles, defies neat definition.

But most people know it when they see it. Or, perhaps more accurately, most of us can point to it when our lives and well-being are disrupted by immature behavior. Townspeople who live in university neighborhoods recount the endless atrocities of noise, all night parties, damage to property, and parking nightmares. Their complaints to university or city officials demand responsible and mature behavior from college students. Whole mini-bureaucracies within the university try to pick up the pieces of student behavior on campus and within the local communities. Increasingly, but without evident consistency, university officials are growing weary of all the behavior problems and are instituting new rules and penalties. But these officials, along with neighborhood residents and the campus police, are up against a formidable culture which resists their efforts to prod or educate students to assume responsibility for their behavior.

In this atmosphere, students who show maturity and embrace some personal responsibility do attract notice. They seem to understand that their choices, actions and inactions will shape their future. Not surprisingly they weigh these actions carefully, surveying the prospects which each choice suggests. They have an instinctive respect for the experience of others who have faced these issues and will consult that experience. Above all, as they glance at all the consequences that are relatively predictable, they do not see themselves as exempt from the dynamics of these choices and their consequences.

Exemption from ordinary and reasonable consequences is the kernel of the American youth syndrome. Flooded with factual information, washed over since early childhood with clever educational messages about lurking dangers, inundated with stories and examples of personal loss or tragedy, a young person is remarkably capable of exempting himself or herself from similar consequences. Young people, of course, have always been notorious for carelessness and for an obliviousness to mortality, but in our culture these very normal adolescent fantasies are purveyed with enormous and attractive effectiveness.

However, reality beckons and sometimes fiercely intrudes itself. Campus ministry needs to examine any of its possible compliance with the unreality of campus life. Religious ministry can also lend itself to the prolonged adolescence, covering itself with a trivial veneer of the dominant youth culture. Our efforts to relate, to be present and relevant to young people, can also contain unhelpful messages of immaturity, in language and symbols which suggest that only momentary feelings are important, or that responsibility is not congenial with spontaneity and creativity. Sometimes the language and image of campus ministries suggest that they are simply another captive of a culture which thrives on unreality.

But students who do worship regularly and form the campus faith communities are, on the whole, searching for more. The steps which lead them to mass or other prayer are already counter-cultural, often as yet without full reflection. Campus ministers are wise to understand the impetus of this youthful searching and to offer an inviting view of reality that will stimulate and encourage those hesitant steps.

7

Prayer, Spirituality and the Bible

When the university medical school concluded a working arrangement with the local Catholic hospitals, the university president hosted a celebration in his home with the archbishop as the guest of honor. At one point, a student, who was working as a waiter at the event, realized that he was offering a tray of food to the archbishop and then promptly got down on one knee to ask for a special blessing for the chemistry final exam he was taking the next day. For a moment, a Catholic archbishop shared the broadest of smiles with a room mixed with atheists, agnostics, skeptics and believers. Everyone enjoyed the moment because everyone in that room had felt exactly what that student, down on one knee, was feeling about his impending exam.

On graduation morning, if the skies are darkly threatening our vast outdoor ceremony, even the most convinced atheists among the faculty will make a point of cheerfully informing the chaplains that we are the people who can do something about the weather. And we all laugh.

Jokes about religious doctrine or deeply held beliefs usually flop because people are anxious and uneasy about doctrine which is always a bit mysterious. But jokes about prayer always work because prayer is something to which nearly everyone can relate. Even when we think it is a bit superstitious, we all know the feelings that prompt a baseball batter to cross himself as he steps to the plate. Public opinion polls reveal that about ninety-four percent of the American people say they believe in God, but that about ninety-six percent say they pray. The experience of saying a prayer is so universal that it evidently does not require belief in the existence of the one to whom we pray. When I remark that the campus chapel is a bit more crowded on the Sunday night just before final exams, the laughter indicates that everyone knows what I'm talking about and enjoys the incongruity of it.

People pray all the time. The most insightful and memorable sermon I have ever heard on the topic was not one which exhorted people to pray but one which skillfully unraveled our lives to reveal that we pray a lot more than we realize. Despite all the efforts of some religious groups to complicate and render the experience esoteric, we continue to pray simply and directly and frequently. Turning to God for help, for guidance, for a moment's respite, is the essence of prayer, reaching fulfillment in our muttered words of thanksgiving. No one has yet improved on the old catechism definition of prayer because it said it so precisely: "The lifting up of the heart and mind to God."

This book argues that our society, including the church, makes too much of the fact that some members of the human race are college students or young people, separating them from the common experience of other human beings when, in fact, they are very much like the rest of people. Nowhere is that more evident than in the realm of prayer. Like everyone else, college students pray, and they pray in much the same way as everyone else.

At Sunday mass I invite the student congregation to add their own spoken petitions to the prayers of the faithful. Sometimes it goes on for many minutes. Someone prays for an aunt with cancer, someone for a sister about to have a baby, someone for a friend who is troubled, someone for the peace talks in the current global hot spot. The prayers are almost always for someone else, keeping the urgent ones for oneself taste-fully private. Of course people acknowledge that God already knows the problem and does not need to be informed. The urge to speak out and to ask others to join in the prayer is too deep within the human soul to be stifled by rational inhibi-tions or modern sophistries. It is the profoundly satisfying moment of handing the urgent concern to the one who is love itself and of entering once again into the trust that prayer makes real.

Students pray for all the same reasons everyone else does, except they do it according to the idiosyncracies of the academic calendar. They pray because they feel the vital con-nection with the divine in their lives. However random and superficial their attention may be, they want more of that connection because they have already experienced its power. Prayer is not something they have to be told about.

SPIRITUAL REALITIES, SUPERNATURAL WORLD

At the beginning of one school year, students who have been providing music at our Sunday masses tell me they would like to add some new pieces to their musical reper-toire. We agree to visit a local Catholic bookstore which has a large selection of music and tapes. On the way I mention that this store also has the best selection of books in the areas of religion and theology in the area. After spending some time selecting music and tapes, I tell them that I want to take a look around in the book section before we leave, and we all wander off in different directions in the large store. When I finish my browsing through new theology titles, I look around to find the students. They are all gathered in a section of books devoted to apparitions, saints and miracles, a section that I nearly always bypass on my visits to this store. As I join them, I see that they are looking through the latest books on the Medjugorge apparitions with great interest. On the ride back to campus, they pepper me with questions about the apparitions at Medjugorge, cures at Lourdes and the pilgrimage of the Pope to Fatima to thank the Virgin Mary for saving his life when he was shot in St. Peter's Square in 1981. These are students who typically feign a weary skepticism about pronouncements from university officials and other authority figures. But there is no skepticism in their interest in miracles, cures and supernatural events. These are students who could take apart a massive mainframe computer and repair it with skill or spend hours telling me everything I ever wanted to know about the intricacies of DNA. But now they seem to have no problems believing that the world of the supernatural intersects with the world of everyday life. In fact, as they talk, they seem convinced that things like this have happened to them.

The least contested elements in Christianity, even in this presumed scientific and technological age, are those which require the greatest leap of faith. Conversations with students who describe themselves as "questioning their faith" or as "former Catholics" usually revolve around personal struggles with specifics of moral doctrine or some scandalizing or alienating personal experience with a church figure. Rarely will these students doubt or question the existence of God, the whole unseen realm of the supernatural, or the human capacity to communicate with that world through prayer. Even among those who are immersed in a logical or scientific worldview, the existence and relevance of the unseen world of the spiritual is apparently more easily accepted than less central and more mundane traditions or teachings. Underlying this pattern there is a widespread recognition that people have had experience of this unseen world in their own lives.

The research of Andrew Greeley shows that a very high

percentage of people say that they have had a religious experience. Conversations with students of all types of religious
affiliation confirm these findings. The influence of a spiritual
world, leaving aside the endless questions about whether it is
coincidence or auto-suggestion, is something which people
can point to in their own experiences. The reality of the
spiritual requires little argument and may, in fact, be the most
self-evident dimension of religion, while being the element at
the farthest remove from any demonstrable process of verification. I hear students speak about the spiritual world with
more confidence and certitude than about any other aspect
of their religious life.

In addressing this dimension of the life of the spirit, in
sermons, retreats and personal conversations, campus ministers are actually inviting young people to stand on familiar
ground. Students look for signals that campus ministers also
revere the world of the spirit and have some familiarity with
it. It is what they expect of us. Yet they are also leery of
religious figures who are uncomfortable or dissmissive of the
supernatural world, and they tend to probe us to find out how
willing we are to acknowledge what they have in fact experienced.

Religion drained of its supernatural perspective soon col-
lapses into a mechanistic strategy of human improvement
which first empties church pews and then becomes indistinguishable from a host of other human self-help techniques.
The evidence that this one-dimensional religion succeeds
only in arousing massive indifference abounds throughout
American society, and nowhere more abundantly than on a
college campus.

Like hundreds of other terms, spirituality now suffers
from the excesses of popularity. As with other over-used and
over-wrought words, we need to recognize that, if everything
is spiritual, then nothing is spiritual. In campus parlance, it is

fashionable to use spirituality to describe all sorts of feelings of connectedness, including the excitement of new ideas and instant feelings of solidarity with constantly changing groups. It may be too late to reclaim its use for the experience of being in relationship to God and the world of graced realities, but it is also important to understand its constant usage as an effort, largely by people unconnected with religious traditions, to appropriate for themselves what they perceive that religion provides for believers. If you cannot or will not come close to the religious traditions, at least you can have some of the same feeling from other sources, usually thought to be more enlightened.

Yet another more polemical use of the term "spirituality" seeks to oppose it to institutional religion which is perceived as sterile and rigid. This usage is rooted in an argument against religion by appealing to the results of religion in people's lives. In fact, many argue, traditional religions are no longer able to supply the power of true spirituality. Other sources are now offered for the experience of the spiritual: ecology, feminism, goddess worship, politics and a syncretic amalgam loosely described as "new age religion." Occasionally people will witness to their experience of finding a kind of spirituality in these movements that they had not been able to find in their traditional religious backgrounds. The media usually features these movements as something new in a field that is often dominated by the familiar and conventional. The spirituality which is presented here is most often a sense of solidarity or bonding around an issue or a new enthusiasm which is almost inherently transitory. There is little evidence, however, that these movements are very significant either on campus or in society as a whole, as was confirmed by the large-scale study on religion in America published by the Graduate School of the City University of New York in April 1991.

SPIRITUALITY AND THE TWELVE-STEP PROGRAMS

A much more important development in the usage of the term "spirituality" is its association with the benefits of the many twelve-step programs dealing with addiction or the effect of someone else's addiction. Individuals in these programs frequently talk about the spiritual nature of the disease of addiction, meaning that, along with its physical and psychological factors, addiction corrodes the life of the spirit. In twelve-step recovery programs people often discover not only a cessation of their addictive use of drugs and alcohol, but also a powerful spiritual renewal which permeates their whole lives. In many cases there is a return to the religious practice which was often abandoned in the course of active addictive behavior.

The twelve-step programs, all of which are the offshoots of the original Alcoholics Anonymous program, are strongly imbued with a spiritual process in which addictive persons "surrender" or "turn over" their disease to God or a higher power. While all twelve-step programs avoid the language of a specific sectarian or denominational tradition, these programs have obviously harnessed the tradition that speaks of God's will and the need to turn one's will over to that divine will.

A growing number of college students have had some experience with twelve-step programs in dealing with a problem of alcohol or drug addiction in their families, usually of a parent. In some instances the whole family has participated in the recovery of a parent, and the children have used the twelve steps to cope with their own lives in this process. Less frequently, young people on their own initiative have sought out the help of a twelve-step program in dealing with a parent's still active addiction. Much less frequently, a student has sought help for his or her own problems with alcohol or drugs, which is understandable in light of the need for most addicts to reach a certain "bottom" before seeking help. Most young people, with their health and energy still fully intact, do not reach such a high or low bottom for some years to come.

Directly or indirectly, through family or friends, greater numbers of students are now aware of the spirituality of twelve-step recovery and the process of healing they offer. Most religions have long seen the remarkable effect of these programs and often provide hospitality, in church meeting halls, for these programs, while at the same time respecting their non-denominational nature. Campus ministers need to be familiar with these programs, not only for referral purposes, but to understand the inner life of growing numbers of students. Speaking to the spiritual experience of recovery programs from a Christian perspective can enrich the spiritual experience that more and more young people have had within these programs, while at the same time illustrating their compatibility with Christian life. Students who have seen first-hand the spiritual power of the twelve-step programs will frequently enter more deeply into Christian worship and practice when they understand that the underlying insights are common to both recovery and traditional Christianity.

THE SPIRITUAL CENTERPIECE

In the following chapter I will be discussing the role of worship in the lives of students, but we might pause here to locate Sunday mass at the center of spirituality for most Catholic students. Everything they have absorbed about Catholicism while growing up points to the mass as the culmination of the life of the spirit which, while also permeating all the dimensions of life, is most focused in the eucharistic celebration. The blending of the highly personal with the community experience, all in the familiar context of ritual worship, has the enduring power of the holy place or holy time, regularly set aside for one's attention to God.

RETREATS

The most lasting religious experience of many students prior to coming to college is the youth retreat sponsored by their high school or youth ministry program. Most teenagers feel that they exist at the margins of typical American parish life with its emphasis on older people, families or very small children. The youth retreat often provides them with their first experience of community and ownership within the larger Christian community. Going away from routine surroundings, being together with people their own age, usually led by people who are especially sensitive to the world of the teenager, the youth retreat leaves a deep and lasting imprint on young people.

These retreats are skillfully organized to precipitate an open sharing of the feelings and emotions which are precisely the source of most teenage angst, leaving a memorable impression of perhaps the first or only time a teenager was able to express feelings in a safe and affirming atmosphere. The tie between this very important emotional opening up and religious faith establishes a highly personal and vivid sense of God and community. Talking with them later in college, one can sense how deeply formative these retreats are in their religious consciousness because retreats serve as a constant reference point whenever faith or religion is the topic. Whether conducted through a Catholic high school or through a parish and/ or diocesan youth ministry program, the retreats constitute the foundational religious experience for many young people. The parish and even the Catholic high school do not touch teenagers on any comparable level.

For about a year after arriving on a college campus, many students want to recapture this earlier experience but are often frustrated because they are also experiencing the passing of the teenage atmosphere which made these retreats so powerful. Even when they participate in the retreats offered through campus ministry, they often have great difficulty duplicating that earlier experience with all its intensity and novelty. The students with whom they are now sharing a college retreat will have had different previous experiences or will be older and less attuned to this sort of teenage interaction. And they discover that, like most of our important early experiences, this one cannot really be repeated.

Campus ministers who are aware of the significance of this earlier retreat experience will be careful to offer a different kind of retreat so as not to seem to be promising what just cannot happen a second time. But more importantly, campus ministers will be alert to build on this earlier formative experience by recalling the earlier impact of community, prayer and the life of the spirit and by showing how these memories can grow into a newer, more adult faith. College level retreats also become central religious experiences, incorporating the teenage experiences in the larger context of the difficult and painful transition to adulthood which is, in turn, central to the college experience.

The popularity of retreats, at all stages of life, is evident testimony to the widespread desire to join highly personal issues to the faith experience, while creating a living continuum among one's personal relationships with other people and one's relationship with God. Looked at from a slightly different perspective, this is the perennial search for the wisdom and grace which can be experienced as strength and motivation in the business of life itself. As already mentioned, when students perceive this connection being made in the life of another student, their curiosity is stirred and they make some effort to find it for themselves. It is often precisely this curiosity that leads a student to sign up for a retreat. That is why it is so useful to have students as leaders on retreats where they can illustrate in their own terms how their faith works and why it makes their lives richer.

THE APPEAL OF FUNDAMENTALISM AND THE BIBLE

I had quickly said, "Of course," when Jim casually asked me if I'd be willing to talk with two of his friends who were having difficulties with the Catholic Church. My mind scanned the list of the usual suspects for such difficulties: sexual morality, the pope, abortion or, especially since the two friends were female, the ordination of women. When Jim added that he had quite a bit of difficulty in dealing with their objections, I felt even more confident in my mental predictions of what they would want to talk about. I could not have been more mistaken, although I should have detected a large clue in his suggestion that we meet in a local coffee shop rather than my office because his friends would probably be upset at the religious icons in my office.

The four of us had barely shaken hands and sat down in the coffee shop when simultaneously both young women reached into their book bags to retrieve large Bibles which they spread out on the table, revealing many passages highlighted in yellows, blues and pinks. I quickly began to realize that abortion was not going to be the issue. Pointing to the passage where Jesus enjoins his followers to "call no man father except your Father in heaven," they informed me that, in accordance with the word of God, they would call me "Pastor Hunt" instead of "Father Hunt." Next out of the book bags came biblical concordances which, as they explained, had references to every word in the Bible and that the words "pope," "immaculate conception," "absolution," and "the assumption of Mary" appeared nowhere in the Bible. With our go-between, Jim, caught somewhere between an uproarious laugh and curiosity, I tried a few words of explanation about how Catholicism treated the Bible as the word of God along with tradition as a source of Christian development and truth. But this, like everything I said for the next few minutes, only led them to turn quickly to another highlighted passage which they promptly recited at Jim and me. They explained that they had come to realize that the Catholic Church, in which both of them had been raised, was only the work of human corruption and that they had discovered the truth of God's word in the Bible, and only in the Bible. We had reached an impasse, and I settled back to listen to them until I could politely excuse myself, but not before learning that the icons on my office walls, as well as statues and stained glass windows in many Catholic churches, were blasphemous contradictions of the commandment against graven images. As we left the table, they assured me that they would pray for me, as they pray for others who have not yet accepted Jesus as their Lord and Savior and the Bible as his word. It was a complete impasse, with no great harm done, except that Jim still to this day delights in calling me "Pastor Hunt."

The growing appeal of biblical fundamentalism on many college campuses over the last few decades has a number of significant dimensions, not always equally present: (1) the security and simple clarity of fundamentalism in an otherwise chaotic and turbulent culture; (2) the energy and manifest devotion of fundamentalists in recruiting and spreading the word; (3) the vacuum left in our still largely Protestant culture by the decline of non-fundamentalist Protestant churches, especially on campus; (4) the ignorance and naiveté of many Catholics about the Bible and how to understand it within the church community; (5) the strong appeal of a message that is not confused with ambiguity and nuance; (6) the boredom and restlessness of many Catholics and mainline Protestants with what they have experienced as excessive or empty ritual; (7) the abiding importance of the Bible in American culture since Plymouth Rock (an importance probably not found in any other culture); finally, (8) the important presence of Bible-centered, fundamentalist Christianity at the core of the American experience, with its revivals and preachers, though not very well noticed by the major media until fundamentalists became politically active with the Moral Majority and other organizations in the 1970s and early 1980s.

These factors serve to illustrate that biblical fundamentalism is neither new nor alien to our society, but the strong profile it has on many campuses and among young people is largely due to the repudiation of modernity which fundamentalism embodies. Rejecting the confused and lax morality of our age, strongly opposing scientific and literary methods of understanding the Bible, firmly repudiating Darwinism in all its forms, and emphasizing the personal witness of its followers, contemporary biblical fundamentalism becomes a magnet for those who are alarmed by what modern American society has become. Some young people despair of the compromises and accommodations which their own churches have made with modern culture and, seeing in these compromises an ever decreasing reliance on the Bible as the inerrant word of God, turn to fundamentalist groups for the clarity and surety of their position. This movement toward biblical fundamentalism, especially in certain parts of the United States, is clearly of significance for all campus ministers, but it is also often both misunderstood and exaggerated in its reach.

Contemporary fundamentalism exhibits two powerful and attractive components: (1) a revival of the Bible as the inerrant word of God and the guide to life; (2) a diagnosis joined with a repudiation of modernity. When fundamentalist groups appear to be making inroads into other campus congregations, especially Catholic or non-fundamentalist Protestant ones, campus ministers often immediately respond with a flurry of their own form of Bible study or classes. Unfortunately, the two ways of understanding the Bible are so incompatible that each group feels confirmed in its own approach. The use of modern literary scientific or literary tools in analyzing the Bible only proves to the fundamentalists that they are right in their diagnosis of what has gone wrong with many of the churches. The end result is like two people talking at each other in languages utterly incomprehensible to the other, occasionally hurling scriptural passages at each other.

We need to evolve a better catechesis about the Bible, its role in the church community, its creation by the early community, and the marvelous methods available for its study today. In our early religious education programs, sermons, classes and campus ministries, we can unfold the meaning of the Bible as the book of the church, the word of God through human authors, and established as authentic by the church. But responding to the immediate fundamentalist challenge cannot substitute for a deeper and more integrated biblical formation.

Young people are initially attracted by fundamentalism's strong rejection of modern American culture. The Bible alone is not the initial attraction of fundamentalism to young people, and we make a grave mistake by engaging in a war of the Bibles. Many young people, who often have a profound, if unarticulated, uneasiness about the culture in which they must live, move toward fundamentalist groups because they offer an alternative to that culture, along with a rather simplified diagnosis of its ills.

Campus ministers might listen to this uneasiness with serious attention, leaving aside their impatience with the biblical methodology. For here the fundamentalists pose the crucial issue of the relationship of Christ and culture, opting largely for the model of Christ against culture. At the other end of the contemporary religious spectrum are religious ministries which embrace the culture so uncritically that they are indistinguishable from modernity itself, with their interests and agendas largely created by the prevailing culture.

The Catholic tradition (and other Christian churches) surely has elements and practitioners of this frenzied relevance, but the tradition is more comprehensively understood in terms of a Christ often at odds with the prevailing culture, but more profoundly transforming culture. (See Niehbur's *Christ and Culture.*) Our Catholic uneasiness with the culture may well embrace the impatience of fundamentalists with the bankruptcy of personal morals and sleazy public behavior, but it also embodies a social justice perspective which analyzes the culture and seeks to create a just society based on the common good.

To provide an effective counter-balance to fundamentalism, we need to develop our understanding of Christ transforming culture, not hesitating to detail the serious points on which we are estranged from the prevailing culture, yet emphasizing our engagement in that culture and the struggle for its soul. The surest way for us to abdicate our responsibility over to the fundamentalists is to offer little or no alternative to the dominant culture on campus and in society at large. When we lapse into an uncritical embrace of modernity, we are not only untrue to the richness of the Catholic tradition, but today we surrender our credibility, leaving our congregations vulnerable to those who stake out clearer ground of opposition to the prevailing culture. "To be in the world, but not of the world" has long been the tightrope we have tried to navigate. The contemporary challenge of fundamentalism should only lead us to more carefully examine the balance we need to make that precarious navigation.

8

Worship

I interrupt Lynn to ask, "How did you leave the Catholic Church? Was it something you actually decided on and then did?" Lynn, a graduate student in biology, has been telling me how she now wants to return to the Catholic Church, but I am trying to understand how she actually left the church in the first place. Finally, when I pose the question more directly, she sits back and has some difficultly describing her exit from the church. Apologizing for the metaphor, she says it was like not renewing a magazine subscription. "After the expiration date, you keep getting a few issues along with occasional reminders. Then one day you realize you haven't been getting the magazine for a while, but you no longer remember whether you decided to stop the subscription or just carelessly let it lapse. But the magazine just isn't around your house anymore."

Her exit from the church happened the same way until one day she realized she wasn't part of it anymore. Now she has decided to rejoin but is not sure of exactly how she drifted away in the first place. I ask her, continuing the magazine analogy, what would be the religious equivalent of noticing the magazine's absence. "Well mass, of course," she quickly responds, searching to see if I am really serious. "I realized that I had just about completely stopped going to mass." I ask if anything else symbolized her exit, and now she is a bit exasperated with me. "What else could be so clear or important as not going to mass?" she asks me, still wondering what I could have in mind to equal that magnitude. She adds that she has not lived up to the teachings and ideals of the church, pointing out that, when she was a practicing Catholic, she had not always lived up to them either. For those failings, she wants to go to confession, but points out that's not leaving the church. But, she is certain, her two year absence from Sunday mass is just that.

As I noted earlier, many campus ministers would like to nuance and enhance the working definition of a "practicing Catholic" to include doctrinal and social justice elements, but most of our campus congregations would opt for the less complicated measure of attending Sunday mass with some regularity. It is simply what you do when you're a Catholic and want to remain one.

But there is much more here than some lingering sense of obligation (not the most prevalent student virtue) or some hangover of guilt about missing mass (most young people have not heard much about that for the last twenty-five years). It is showing up when you attach importance to something. When Woody Allen says that ninety percent of life is just showing up, he is capturing a universal experience. If you are a union member who values the union, you go to meetings, as do faculty who are involved on campus, and as families who are always showing up at family gatherings whatever the boredom factor. Showing up for mass is what Catholics do about being Catholic.

Students acknowledge that there are many ways of worshiping God but this is the way you combine that worship with the Catholic tradition you have received. It is what you do. Family, friends, the experience of growing up, the memories of all that is intertwined with being Catholic, are all ingredients in the mix of being Catholic and all have a strong association with going to mass. Identity, belonging, self-definition, habit, group awareness, community experience and familiar ways of touching God are all woven into the Sunday mass experience for most Catholics. Even with all the predictable negatives associated with Sunday mass—teenage boredom, bad sermons, getting up too early—it is a powerful dynamic in a young person's life. In a pluralistic society like ours where most people are not Catholic, Sunday mass is also the regular way of locating yourself and your family within that society, which may also explain why Sunday mass attendance is generally higher here than in societies where nearly everyone is Catholic.

Colleagues serving other religious denominations ask me to explain why so many students go to mass. In some denominations high attendance is directly related to great preaching or the minister's charisma or to some unique program offered by the church, and so they naturally are curious to discover what device works to attract so many students. I explain that all I could do is foil the dynamic of attendance and empty out the church by months of really offensive sermons. But even then, I add, many of the students would merely shift their Sunday practice to a local parish, missing the sense of campus community and adding some inconvenience. These discussions with religious colleagues often move on to the old reformation division of emphasis between the word and the sacrament which, while more balanced today on both sides of that reformation divide, is still reflected in our congregations today. Among Catholics, it is the sacrament, far more than the words or charisma of the minister, which gathers the people.

Yet there has been significant change in Catholic expectations—not a lessening of the sacramental attraction, but a greater appreciation of a valuable sermon. I explain to my colleagues that the sermon, while not determining Sunday attendance (unless it is a whole series of abominable sermons), is decisive in determining my ministry for the rest of

the week. Students regularly seek me out for pastoral coun-
selling because something I said in a sermon indicated I was
aware of the kind of problem they were dealing with, or had
some experience which they could utilize, or had a sensitiv-
ity to some issues they have been wanting to talk about. My
choice of examples in a Sunday sermon is predictive of the
kind of conversations I will have with students in coming
weeks. Students do listen to sermons. They will often cite
something I said weeks ago in a sermon which I have already forgotten myself. I have been surprised so often by
their attention to sermons that I now begin my sermon
preparation, after reading the assigned scriptures, by thumb-
ing through my appointment book to refresh my memory
about discussions with students so that I can relate the topics of those discussions to the scriptural truths.

Unfortunately, the Catholic post-reformation devaluation
of the sermon has not yet ended, and many of us still fail to
realize the importance and potential of the sermon. It is the
only glimpse into us as people that most students will ever
get, the only indication they will ever have of whether we
would be approachable or worth approaching. In a mere ten
or fifteen minutes we communicate all that we are going to
be able to communicate to most of our congregations. The
sacrament attracts and is the centerpiece of Catholic life, but
the sermon sets the tone and substance of the ministry. It
would be going too far to suggest that we begin posting sermon topics on signs outside our campus chapels, but a symbolic sign should be posted where the preacher can see it
through the week and be reminded of the awesome responsibility and opportunity which we assume in those few minutes
during Sunday mass.

Campus ministry frequently offers an attractive spectrum
of programs, seminars, Bible study and personal growth
groups for students, in addition to the personal pastoral coun-

seling which constitutes a major part of all campus ministry. These offerings provide a more intense experience of Christian community, a deeper integration of faith with life experience, and serve to form the leaders of the faith community on campus as well as for the future life of the church. But even when such programs are greatly successful, they will touch only a fraction of the entire worshiping community. Human nature, inertia and the hectic demands of university life will keep many, if not most, students from participation in these programs. For these significant numbers, the Sunday worship experience, specifically the quality of the sermon, will be the crucial link with the faith community. Of course, it is not enough, but frequently it is all we have. The preparation and care which we bring to these few moments of contact on Sunday are crucial to the effectiveness of our ministry. Even the other programs will generally rise or fall on the basis of the Sunday experience which serves as the invitation to a fuller participation in the faith community.

Observers of the large numbers at campus mass sometimes ask, "Is that all Catholics are interested in, or need— mass on Sunday?" Even when the question implies a superficiality about Catholic commitment, I respond with a definite "yes." The Sunday eucharist is the beginning and the end of all we do. It is the place where we welcome the first, tentative involvement and where we celebrate the full-blown active Christian life. Liturgists have often, for these very reasons, described the Sunday eucharist as "the source and summit of the Christian life." A note of realism hastily adds that, for many, it is the only definitively Christian event of the week. Each Sunday is both the same thing all over again—and a fresh new beginning.

In the splintering of traditional religious ministries over the past quarter of a century, some have opted for more specialized ministries, focusing on a disenfranchised or marginalized group, or becoming identified with one of the pressing moral issues on campus, often setting aside the call to weekly worship as a lesser priority best left to what are called the "local churches." While much of this specialized ministry has also evolved within the Catholic framework, the centrifugal pull of our sacramental ecclesiology has largely prevented us from abandoning the Sunday congregation. The impetus of Vatican II has served to enhance the centrality of the Sunday eucharist. As a result, nearly all Catholic campus ministries continue to be eucharist-centered which, in addition to being the embodiment of contemporary ecclesial self-understanding, has the very practical benefit of anchoring us in the reality and the challenge of the life of a congregation.

CAMPUS LITURGY

Newman Centers, or campus chapels, uniformly report that they attract numbers of worshipers from the larger community who often have no direct affiliation with the university. Families, older people, and single Catholics often seek out campus centers or chapels largely because they are attracted to the style of worship in campus settings. While this sometimes causes conflict or at least confusion for the role of the ministers who, at some point, must ask whether they are there primarily to serve the student community or the many people "from the outside" who join in the Sunday celebration, this attractiveness of campus worship has important lessons for the whole church.

What is there about campus worshiping communities that sets them apart and makes them, for many, so attractive?

Even at first sight, a visitor is struck by the fact that students show up. A middle-aged believer, weary perhaps of the rote and conventionality of some parish life, is inevitably impressed by that fact that students, obviously under no parental or peer pressure, get to mass entirely on their own. Their youth makes one feel optimistic and hopeful about the future, while at the same time regenerating a sense of confidence in the ancient tradition that is engaging a new generation right before your eyes.

A second factor that sets campus worship apart from much parish life is the turnover of people each year. While such turnover makes stability and continuity more difficult, it almost ensures creativity and freshness. In communities where about twenty-five percent of the students leave each year to be replaced with a similar percentage of new people, there is rarely a decisive argument from the "This is the way we have always done it" vantage point. As any campus minister can testify, this means recruiting new musicians, readers, and other leaders every year, but it does generate new life and energy every year, often every semester.

The lack of the kind of resources found in the more stable parish communities is a third factor which requires campus ministers and campus communities to continually reform and recreate themselves. Frustrating for some, this can mean a constant flow of energy and vitality often less needed and therefore less valued in parish communities.

Finally, campus ministers themselves tend to be the men and women who have most enthusiastically embraced the renewal of the church born at Vatican II. Whether campus ministry attracts people of this temperament, or whether the nature of being the church in a campus setting forges such a temperament, the end result has been that perhaps nowhere else in the church has the reform and renewal of Vatican II been so vigorously implemented as in campus communities. Now, nearly thirty years after the council, the evidence is overwhelming: the council works.

All these factors combine to create a sense of community

ownership, especially ownership of worship. The liturgy is never owned in the sense of the community inventing or reinventing its form of worship each time. If a community embarked on this radical departure, it would also be leaving the Catholic tradition behind. The liturgy belongs to the whole church, but each community has the capacity to make the eucharist its own. In this sense, campus communities of faith often experience the eucharist very much as their worship, coming from their own experience. This is even more likely on campus because most of the members of the faith community will be present without the factors of habit, family/peer influence or sheer conventionality.

In campus worship people experience a sense of belonging to and knowing the community. They usually know, at least on some level, most of the other people with whom they worship. This sense of community is not the same as the intense, more intimate sense of community that people find in small prayer groups, or in Christian base communities, or even in the smaller groups, like the musicians, which are part of the liturgy. Most people will want to meet and get to know the people they worship with, and will value the open and welcoming spirit which enables such meeting, but they are not seeking the intense, intimate closeness which they have already found in their friendships, their social groupings, families or relationships. Sometimes, in campus communities, the leadership can become dominated by people who are eagerly seeking such closeness and intimacy in the worshiping community, often forcing an artificial closeness which can be quite alienating to the larger group. Pastoral leadership needs to be alert to this potential problem by sensitively guiding people to smaller groups within the community which can provide a much better opportunity for closeness and intimate friendship. Liturgy is the prayer of a community and can be wrenched into a kind of distortion when it is made to bear purposes and objectives for which it is not designed. The warmth and hospitality with which a worshiping community welcomes new people is most inviting when it also allows people to find their own levels of friendship and intimacy with their new community.

RECONCILIATION: A DISAPPEARING SACRAMENT?

"But do you ever hear confessions over there anymore?" The pastor of a parish not far from the campus has invited me to speak with the parents of the high school students about college life. Now after the parents have asked a lot of questions about student life, the pastor has returned to his skepticism about my description of the strong Catholic worshiping community on campus. I have already assured him that the chapel on campus is full for mass on Sunday, but he is still wary of the possibility of faith surviving on our campus. Now I try to answer his question about confession. I tell him that it is a qualified yes. Yes—many students do seek confession, but yes—it is very different these days.

Post-Vatican II catechesis has been so successful that most younger Catholics view sin not as the end of their Christian life, but as the opportunity to seek the reassurance of forgiveness. The image of God which they have assimilated is far from the unbending judge of an alleged Catholic past, but rather that of a parent who readily forgives and welcomes those who have strayed. If this generation seems to have less frequent recourse to the sacrament of reconciliation, it is not that they judge themselves perfect and without the need of constant forgiveness. Rather they have heard the message of the modern church, including the messages delivered in the liturgy itself. They have not been taught to fear God or to constantly check, through frequent confession, that they are in a state of grace. In doubt, they have been taught, and learned well, to trust that God forgives. But, above all, in the renewed liturgy, they have heard the forgiveness of God proclaimed, first as the liturgy begins, and a number of other times before communion. They take the liturgy at its word: ". . . only say the word, and I shall be healed."

Many are rediscovering the sacrament of reconciliation, not as it might have been used thirty or forty years ago, but as a time to sit down with a valued confessor to put their judgments about themselves into words and to discuss their lives, problems and doubts. The church has been caught in a dilemma about this once utterly familiar touchstone of Catholic life. On the one hand we effectively proclaim the unconditioned forgiveness of God, and yet perhaps worry about the apparent disappearance of regular confession, while at the same time not very successfully illustrating what a meaningful sacramental encounter of reconciliation might actually be like.

Like many in campus ministry, I frequently have students tell me what a liberating experience the reconciliation encounter has been, but they usually preface it with a disclaimer that they did not know how this could be done. Add to this the natural anxiety which eighteen to twenty-two year olds feel about disclosing themselves to someone who is older and you have the impasse which we all experience about the sacrament of reconciliation. Explaining and actually showing how it can be done is one of the most urgent requirements in contemporary pastoral ministry.

WHY IS MASS SO IMPORTANT ?

"This kid is what? About twenty years old? I'd like to meet him. Boy, the mass is really important to him, isn't it?" A priest friend who served as chaplain on this campus over twenty years ago has been visiting me on the weekend just before the January semester begins on Monday. When I return home from some shopping, he gives me a long telephone message which he took for me while I was out. The caller was the president of the student community calling me from his home in Virginia to let me know that he will be back for the Sunday night mass tomorrow, and his message is full of the details he has taken care of for the first mass of the new semester: the readers, the people to take up the collection, the music group and the refreshments we have after mass. My priest friend tells me that the call was quite a revelation for him, to hear a college student, still at home on vacation, making sure everything is in place for Sunday mass. Shaking his head in wonder, he says, "You just don't expect that these days." Urging him to join us for the mass tomorrow night, I assure him, "You'll see a lot a people there who think it is pretty important."

If regular confession is not as common as it might have once been, the mass itself has not moved off-center. However sophisticated or nuanced a person is with regard to confession, morality, or even theological issues, Sunday mass continues to be the way people identify themselves as Catholics. The rhythms of life require that we pay attention to important relationships in a way that is partially structured, scheduled and very familiar. And so Catholics go to mass, or they stop going and begin to lose their identity as Catholics.

In a pluralistic society like the United States, there is also, I suspect, an added need to identify oneself on the religious spectrum, or conversely to undo one's given identity. Many times I have heard Catholic students respond to questions about why they attend mass in words to the effect: "That's what you do if you're a Catholic." This response, which is fully understandable to Catholics, perplexes and mystifies those who are not from the tradition. In countries where the vast majority of people are Catholic, the need to express one's religious identity is obviously not as common as it is in our society where it functions, along with ethnic and racial factors, as an important identity marker. The role of identity assertion may help to explain why mass attendance seems to be higher here, especially among the young, than in predominantly Catholic countries. International students and faculty from Catholic countries frequently comment on their surprise at finding much greater numbers of young people at mass here than in their home countries. The role of religion in constructing identity is further evidenced for me when I hear American students describe each other. They nearly always know the religious background of another student, even when that background has become tenuous or ambiguous.

Sin or behavior in general does not function as a "cutting off" point for young Catholics because they have confidence in the way back. Their unhappiness and frustration with their own behavior combines with external factors like fierce competition to undermine their self-esteem, but it does not make them feel cut off from the church. Only one's presence or absence at Sunday mass is fraught with such meaning. This constitutes an important sociological and psychological reading of our congregations which, along with the centrality of the eucharist in contemporary church life, defines what should be, and in fact already is, the highest priority of any campus ministry.

WHAT ARE THEY DOING AT MASS?

After a long day of formal meetings with a committee evaluating the structure of religious chaplaincies at the university, the rabbi, the Protestant minister and I have grabbed some refreshments and leaned back to debrief the day's events. Quickly we discover that we are bored rehashing the evaluation meeting and turn to more irreverent topics. After some complaining about the usual problems, we begin sharing some of our own personal questions about ministry.

Pointing at me, the rabbi says, "Michael, I'd like to hear you explain, off the record, why so many students show up at mass on Sunday." Quickly he warns me, "And don't say it's guilt because we Jews are much better at guilt than Catholics could ever be!"

I had been asked so many times to explain why students attend mass that I decided to ask the students themselves. Colleagues in ecumenical ministry, college administrators, faculty and many students who were not Catholic would ask why I thought so many students seemed to defy the popular image of a secular generation. People wonder if Catholic indoctrination about obligation is so effective, or they look for some hidden factor in the mass itself, or they feel compelled to dismiss the phenomenon, saying "It's just that Catholics think they have to go to mass," as if it could be contrasted with some mythical, totally free religious association elsewhere.

As I never felt I was adequately understanding the phenomenon myself and had to admit that I was somewhat surprised myself by the turnout for mass, I asked the question on a brief survey I conducted with students right at mass. I have now done this survey twice in the past eight years with two different generations and asked the same question: "Why do you attend Sunday mass?" Both surveys yielded just about the same response. Over ninety percent each time said they attended mass to pray. Some students added comments about the parts of the mass which they valued most, or indicated the importance of mass in their families, or mentioned that they had just begun attending since coming to college. But the clear dynamic at work is prayer.

From this response I conclude that we frequently read both too much and too little into student mass participation. I say too much because the response does seem to indicate that we ought not to assume too much about students at mass in terms of their theological level of formation. They are at mass, not because they have assimilated or worked out a coherent personal religious worldview, but rather, more directly, they have come to pray in a way they have become familiar with. And I suggest that we can read too little into their attendance by not fully absorbing the strong indictment which their participation makes about the prevalent secular stereotypes of our society, especially of the young.

"Let us pray," the frequent invitation issued by the celebrant at Catholic liturgy, turns out to have a precise accuracy both in terms of what the service is about and what the congregation thinks it is doing.

I have also asked individual students to say more about their responses on these questionnaires—among other things, asking them why they do not just pray in the privacy of their own time and space. Invariably when prompted to say more about their practice of attending mass to pray with others, they cite some measure of community importance, the sense of well-being it conveys and some notion of an obligation to be present. However, their sense of obligation is far removed from the dour obligation or fear of divine punishment that allegedly marked earlier generations.

Students do express a sense of obligation in terms of being attentive to something they hold important, mingled with a realistic fear, not of divine retribution, but of easily losing something important by treating it carelessly. Just as they already know full well that friendships and relations with family will diminish when the visits or phone calls become infrequent or non-existent, they know that their relationship with God atrophies when they neglect it by not showing up.

They may not feel or expect every Sunday mass to convey the same heightened spiritual awareness, but they are confident already that their absence will put distance between themselves and God.

If the majority of students at mass are there for something as uncomplicated but as profound as prayer, we need to exercise great care to make certain that we are gathered to pray. We need to be unambiguous about the purpose of this gathering in the way we conduct it and invite participation.

It requires that we simultaneously note the routine character of what we have come to do, while tending to a sense of awe at the one whom we are addressing and the clarity of purpose which draws people to respond to our invitation, "Let us pray."

9

Catholic Identity

The Catholic practice of abstaining from meat on Fridays was originally meant to commemorate the day of the Lord's death in a sacrificial way. The church rule on Friday abstinence from meat was taken with great seriousness, at least in many parts of the church. By the time I was old enough to observe the practice of meatless Fridays, it had lost most of its sacrificial character, as Catholics, at least in countries like the United States, could have a wonderful seafood dinner to observe the Friday discipline. The times had obviously changed and accordingly, in the 1960s, the church relaxed the rule, making the Friday observance purely optional. The change inspired a memorable cartoon in *The New Yorker* in which a perplexed devil wonders what to do with all the inmates who had earned a place in hell for eating meat in Friday. Was the change retroactive?

Although it was clear that the Friday tradition had long lost its penitential meaning, most failed to see at the time that it had been transformed from a sacrificial observance to a badge of Catholic identity, especially in places where most people were not Catholic. Letting a host know in advance that you could not eat meat, declining a hot dog at a baseball game, discreetly alerting dinner companions to your perusal of a menu in search of fish—all these served to proclaim something important about yourself. It said symbolically, "I am a Catholic and it's important to me." It was the one of the things non-Catholics all knew about us. We did not eat meat on Fridays. It had a very vivid, public aura about it and was usually respected by non-Catholics because, along with the use of Latin, it was one of the few things that "others" knew about us. Those who were less friendly to the church referred to Catholics as "mackerel snappers," because our Friday custom was so well known.

There are no comparable badges of identity for young Catholics today.

Earlier in the book I referred to the massive turnout of students for mass on Ash Wednesday every year, citing the powerful symbolism of the taking of ashes. But I also think the response is due, in part, to the very distinctive Catholic character of the taking and wearing of ashes on the forehead. While some other Christian denominations have the practice, it is one of those few things that is very distinctively Catholic. If you walk around campus with ashes rubbed on your forehead on that day, you are wearing a badge that tells everyone something important about yourself. Ash Wednesday is not a day of obligation in church law, but more students will come on that day than any other in the year to take one of the few distinctively Catholic emblems.

The content and style of Catholic identity has changed greatly in recent years, but I want to suggest that the desire for that identity, especially among college students, is strong and persistent.

The Newman movement, or campus ministry, began as a concern for preserving the Catholic identity of those students who attended colleges and universities where that identity could easily be lost. In the early years of this century, the concern for Catholic identity was also joined with an effort to provide social occasions for Catholic students to meet each other and to lessen the possibilities of mixed marriages (which were, in those days, seen as another threat to Catholic identity). A glance at the programs and brochures of Newman Clubs of that era will reveal the strong emphasis on shoring up the Catholic identity and social life of students at secular institutions.

The apologetics and ecclesiology of the times lent a dramatic urgency to these efforts. The Catholic Church was "the one, true church." Remaining in the church, and enabling people to remain, had an eternal significance. The salvation of souls was at stake. All Catholics of that era, including students, had a host of distinctively Catholic emblems: the Latin language, the Friday abstinence, the midnight fasting for communion, the detailed Lenten observances, the refusal to share in non-Catholic worship, even when it was Christian, all blended with varying measures of defensiveness and arrogance. When I describe such practices in a survey course on Catholicism, all students find them fascinating. The students who are Catholic feel some relief that these customs no longer survive, but they also display a wistful appreciation of what these customs asserted and often wonder what replaced them.

The changing times and the theology of Vatican II, especially its recognition of the inherent Christian values in other denominations, have made these emblems largely obsolete. The urgency, once tinged with eternal consequences, to keep people Catholic has receded as we have gradually allowed God to work his grace beyond the clear perimeters of the Catholic Church. Few if any Catholic campus ministers today would see allegiance and membership within the church as the end of their efforts, but rather see the church, as it describes itself, as a means to an end, the kingdom, which is not yet realized on this earth.

But the richness of post-Vatican II ecclesiology leaves unanswered questions which pose themselves more psychologically than theologically. "Is it important to be a Catholic?" "Is it of decisive importance?" "Is it just yet another way of being Christian?" "Does it enter into important decisions like marriage, the raising of children, and family values?" "Is there anything distinctive about being Catholic?"

Clearly, being Catholic is important to many college students who, lacking the clarifying emblems of earlier generations, search for some adequate form of identity. And clearly being Catholic is important for campus ministers who, without fully understanding why, know that, if they offered some generic Christian substitute for Catholic worship, they would be facing nearly empty chapels.

The shaping of new forms of Catholic identity, especially in a religiously pluralistic society like ours, requires that attention be given to both the interior life which we share in word and sacrament and to the public witness we give to gospel values in our society. The Catholic Worker Movement and groups like the Jesuit Volunteers provide contemporary models which integrate the inner personal religious motivation of members with a distinctive Catholic service to the larger society. As many college students seek opportunities to serve in groups like these, campus ministry and student leaders are shaping new forms of Catholic identity, new and surely more lasting emblems of the faith we share.

CONCERN FOR CATHOLIC IDENTITY

If remaining a Catholic is no longer equated with an exclusive entree to eternal salvation, why be concerned? If people can find God in a myriad of ways, why all the effort and energy to build up and nurture Catholic communities of faith on campus, or anywhere for that matter? While it is true that most people do not think eternal salvation is at stake, many are concerned, students included, about "being Catholic."

Parents frequently hope that their children will continue

to be Catholic and wonder what will happen when they see their children off to college. Most parents today are wise enough to know that they can be counter-productive, pushing and inquiring too much about the issue, but hoping nonetheless. Some parents decide to avoid completely questions about religious practice once the child has gone off to college, looking for some hint or indication in a chance conversation. Some, as always, lean too heavily on the issue, provoking a youthful assertion of independence, on this as on many other parental desires. Some students will eagerly let their parents know they have dropped religious observance, knowing that such knowledge can be a lethal punishment for a variety of resentments.

Ellen returned to her religious practice about the middle of her senior year after abandoning it as a sophomore. She was quick to tell me that her devout mother was so happy that she had resumed attending Sunday mass. I ask her, "How did your mother know that you had stopped going to mass? Did you tell her?" "Not really," she explains, "but I would often call home to say hello at 10:30 or so on Sunday night, and, of course, my mother knew that was mass time and I wasn't there." In my mind I think of the clever way she had of getting back at her mother for a host of reasons.

At a special mass for parents' weekend each year, I make a point of describing the large turnout of students there is for Sunday night mass on campus. I see the faces of the parents light up with real delight, knowing that what is important to them is being carried on to another generation. As we mingle socially after the mass, I see the greater delight in parents' faces if they realize their son or daughter knows me from regular Sunday mass. A son or daughter introduces me by my name and says something that clearly indicates we already know each other well from Sundays. Parents in that moment quickly realize that the son or daughter, now on their own and away from home, is keeping the faith alive. For many parents, that moment of instant realization is the greatest gift they could have received. Yet there are others who realize that the son or daughter has never met me before. In the eyes of the student I can see the anxiety as they wonder if this priest is going to come right out and say it, "Nice to meet you" (implied, "for the first time"). I never do, of course, but I can see that the parents know full well it is the first time and the son or daughter is only there because the parents have come. No, the parents are not worried about eternal salvation, but they feel the sadness of something being lost.

Parents capture best the core meaning of the concern for Catholic identity because they, at least many of them, are constantly seeking to pass on to their children what they have valued in their own lives. From mundane, common sense wisdom to lofty personal insights, the cumulative experience of parents is offered with love and not a little apprehension to the next generation. The anxiety that most parents suffer revolves around the techniques and methods for communicating their wisdom. Sensitive parents know that too much or too little eagerness can alienate and that they must often wait for the right time to talk about what they have learned in life. Needless to say, many parents today speak from a wisdom earned through their own difficulties with divorce, single parenting and other dislocations of family life. But these parents, perhaps more than others, believe that they have a lot to share with their children, often in the hope that their own mistakes will not be easily repeated.

Those of us who work with young people can gain great insight by examining the inner struggle of parents to pass on what is valuable to their children. In its resolute capacity to care, parental love has no analogue in human experience.

Parents, whether married, divorced or remarried, have often found a great reservoir of strength, comfort and sheer endurance in their Catholic faith. Though they themselves may have drifted away from that faith when younger, they require no demonstration of its essential support and value. From their vantage in life, they know that their college-age children have not yet faced the life issues which drive a person back to the most fundamental resources, but they want that faith to be there for their children when that time does come and when they may no longer be there. Spend any time with the Catholic parents of college students and you will quickly see how important the transmission of that legacy is to their unfinished role as parents. These are not parents who are rigid and controlling, or who panic over college-age religious rebellions, but they want to make sure that they leave to their children something to come back to when the time comes for digging in and depending on what is lasting and basic as they have probably done themselves. Their hope has nothing of the abstract or theoretical about it. They know what gives people the strength to deal with disappointments, family problems, illness and death.

These, of course, are the parents a campus minister is likely to meet at a parents' weekend mass or who will take the time to introduce themselves to chaplains on campus. A significant number of parents are as indifferent about their faith as any college student. They do not know what to tell their children about religious faith and a host of other values. The confusion and turmoil of families today has made many parents and children indifferent to a host of values, including religious faith. The results of this turmoil and indifference are manifest on a college campus.

But those parents who know and care provide us with the core of what we used to call apologetics, reasonable arguments for the validity of the faith perspective. Not proof but reasonable arguments. They know faith works. It has worked for them and they want that to be there for their children.

The most compelling reason for students' religious practice is when they discern this in their parents, perhaps also grandparents, and want it for themselves. When students are able to get by the adolescent conflicts and the rituals of self assertion, they decide that nothing else they have come across does what their parents' faith has done. Times and customs change but the need to have that grounding never disappears. And students of such parents fill our campus chapels for Sunday mass. They are joined there by other students, whose own parents may well be religiously indifferent, because these students have seen it in others and want it for themselves.

This seeking for Catholic identity is not driven by a desire to be superior or even better than others but rather by the perennial need to be specific, to give it a name, to locate it in time and space, to be a Catholic and to say so.

Our campus ministry needs to be unambiguously Catholic, without exclusiveness or arrogance, but with clarity. We have a history from which we have learned some things that must be told. We are not novices in the experiences of this earth. People have faced things before. Their stories need to be told in the community of faith. There are difficulties and confusions in being a Catholic. But the comfort is the knowledge that we are not the first people to have faced the dilemmas of life, and in Jesus Christ we have communion with all those who also believed in him.

WILL THERE BE CATHOLICS IN THE FUTURE?

The question has more than a mere hypothetical flavor for many in ministry today. At times I have felt the question posed by the culture, especially that of young people, which seems at least oblivious to the presence of religion. People I talk with on campus often assume that most religion, especially Catholicism, is fading from the scene in contemporary America. Sometimes an article in the press or on a television news program draws similar conclusions. It is a common-place to speak of a past, and only a past, when religion and church influenced people. Conversations with other campus ministers frequently reveal the prevalence of such assumptions even among those working in the church.

The question is more poignant when a parent, or a teacher, or a pastor detects the disappearance in the next generation of what they tried to pass on. Usually the question is not stated as baldly as I did at the beginning of this section, but it exists as a low-grade doubt, casting a cloud of a certain sadness and feeling of uselessness. In the anxieties and concerns of parents, teachers and pastors, you can hear the unspoken but very real question: "Why am I doing all these things when everyone seems to be giving it up?"

The perception is real. When graduating seniors seemed very confused about the order of a very secularized baccalaureate service which is held on graduation weekend, a vice president commented to me that "these students are lost at a ceremony like this because they have never been in a church or synagogue." But my perception of the confusion was very different, because I saw dozens of faces familiar to me from regular Sunday mass. I concluded that they were confused at what to do because a secularized, non-religious service is just not part of anybody's experience. Yet I know that many people would nod agreement to the vice president's declaration of the death of religion.

At times I have the same perception, but I also know that large numbers do respond. I recognize the truth in the public opinion polls that indicate the strong role of religion, God, prayer and religious motivation in the lives of people. Yet sometimes I just wonder if the "end" has been delayed in our case and wait with apprehension for the next semester when we will experience it with full force. But that never happens. In our Sunday campus congregation, the twenty-five percent who graduate and move on are always replenished with an equal number of new students. But still the apprehension remains. Maybe we have been given another year's reprieve.

Altogether the questions can create a crisis of confidence. Some campus ministers decide that the church or tradition which they represent has lost its capacity to gather young people, and they offer themselves as resources for the university community without any reference to church community-building. And in some cases it does appear that once-strong traditions can no longer form a worshiping community. But even here, more questions remain. Does this happen because the ministers have already decided themselves that gathering a community of faith and worship is an anachronism and moved on to other tasks? Which comes first? Did religion die out, or was the call to gather in worship abandoned?

The Catholic tradition has made it nearly impossible to neglect completely the call to worship, but the uncertainty about the future persists. Not surprisingly, this confusion has generated a new form of clarity. Cultural Catholics are distinguished from committed Catholics, and the former, when seeking marriage or the baptism of a child, are sometimes turned away. The distinction has real validity but in young people it can be a very difficult distinction to render with clarity.

A young married couple who had both been very much a part of our campus community were recently invited to be godparents at the baptism of a new niece. The parish where the baptism was to take place required that they send a letter from their pastor indicating their status as practicing Catholics. But this couple had moved three times in the same city within the last year and a half, and no parish would give them such a letter unless they had been regular members of the parish for at least a year. Fortunately, a few phone calls solved the problem, but not before it had come close to being a profoundly alienating experience for two young Catholics whose mobile lives did not fit the desired clarity.

The desire for this near absolute clarity surely flows from our own insecurities about the future, wishing that a new set of regulations will rescue us from our worries and anxieties. These new regulations also have within them an ingrained suspicion of people, in part because we write off people, especially the young, thinking they have little or no real religious or Catholic allegiance. We do not expect them to be Catholic, real Catholics, anymore.

Yet, on campus, that is why they gather with us. Because they are Catholics. We need to nurture that identity by talking about it, by unfolding its meaning and history, and especially by inviting people to share it with others. The identity is there already, but we need to affirm and celebrate the matchless dimension of the mystery of Christ which it embodies for millions in the world today as it has for long centuries.

Above all, each campus minister needs to communicate that it is important to him or her to be a Catholic. Overreacting to the triumphalism and arrogance of the past, some have relegated that importance to a hidden background. When we do this, we are failing to meet the needs of those for whom we minister and, while receiving applause and approval of the secular-minded for this reticence, we render our ministry ineffective.

The future is impenetrable but it is demonstrably not a bleak future. There will be Catholics in the future because so many college students practice their faith now. They will change and move in different and unpredictable directions. But something which today has the extraordinary capacity to gather so many young people in faith and worship will not become "a thing of the past."

10

The Church on Campus: Campus Ministry

Students active in Catholic campus communities are usually very much aware of differences between ministry—and the ministers—on campus and what they experienced in a parish back home. Same church, but usually very different pews. Most of these differences result from the uniqueness of campus life, but frequently students ask how campus ministry arrived at this point.

Those of us who work with students in these same faith communities are always alert to knowing students and their concerns, but some reflection on who we are and where we have come from can have comparable importance for our ministry. Occasionally pausing to collect our thoughts and to attempt some self-understanding enhances the whole community we serve on campus. Understanding the students with whom we work is a two way street, and we need to invite students to understand us, our ministry and the vision which guides us, as well as the difficulties and frustrations which are specific to campus ministry.

"Marginal people" and "marginal ministry" were the favorite terms with which Catholic campus ministers described themselves and their ministry for many years. Although they may have mirrored the excessive introspection and self-concern of the period, these terms have much validity. The campus minister functions at the edge of two institutions, both of which are very busy about things other than campus ministry. The "sending institution," the church or the diocese, is normally preoccupied with issues around parishes, Catholic Charities, schools and religious education. The church sends men and women to work on secular campuses, hoping they can do some good, but not expecting a grcat deal because of the age of the students and the atmosphere of the secular university. The "receiving institution," the college or university, usually accepts campus ministers as another resource available on campus, but, having foresworn any religious purpose, does not expect or desire religious ministry to be very central to the life of the university. Most campus ministers, however effective their ministry, have felt very much at the edge of the church and its concerns, no less than they were at the edge of the real concerns of the university.

Living at the margins of both the church and the university, often lacking dependable resources, coping with long and erratic hours, and facing a new situation each year can take an exacting toll on campus ministers. Some thrive in this situation, but some burn out or grow frustrated while yearning for more orderly and stable ministries. Yet these very difficult circumstances have also provoked enormous creativity and brilliant ministries.

The inherent unreality of much of academic life impacts on campus ministry, causing it to limit its perspective to the small world of even the largest university. The issues and concerns which loom large on campus can consume people in that community but have little or no corresponding importance in the larger, "real world." To some extent, campus ministry is prone to being isolated from the larger church and its concerns. But at its best, campus ministry acts as a conduit between the often isolated worlds, bringing a measure of the reality of the larger church, and the larger world, into the campus environment. Effective campus ministry also reaches out on behalf of the university community to assist people to comprehend the campus which, in many cases, is poorly understood.

Campus ministry also experiences the mixed blessing of the frequent and substantial turnover of its congregations. Every four or five years, an entirely different congregation replaces the one that has graduated or found a better teaching position. Draining as this experience can be, it also leads to many fresh starts and guarantees a perennial flexibility.

The personal demand for counseling, especially with students, can be difficult to manage. Newcomers to campus ministry quickly learn to forget all their neat assumptions about time and scheduling when working with students who will show up willing to talk and unburden themselves spontaneously at almost any moment but who will also completely forget appointments for the same. Student lives are measured out on two different calendars, one which governs the "real world" and one which is divided into semesters or quarters with exams and papers due, but most students do not navigate either calendar with much precision. Coping with the schedule, or lack of schedule, of student life can be very unnerving unless the campus minister fully recognizes the inevitable confusion in advance.

In the midst of all this, campus ministers set out to create and build a Catholic faith community which, by necessity, will lack some of the parts of such a community. There may be no one else in the community over thirty years of age. Or friendly local middle-age people may join in the campus community but threaten (in a friendly manner) to consume the campus minister's time and energy.

The usual resources of established and proven leadership may be totally lacking, and the physical sites for worship and other programs may be constantly shifting. Yet in most cases, the campus community of faith thrives and follows its own laws of growth and change.

Most campus faith communities are deprived of the role of the different generations in the full faith experience. Students who worship regularly on campus may not see young children who are beginning their Christian life, nor have much contact with older people whose lives evidence a tested Christian strength. Programs with the community like tutoring and visiting nursing homes can add something of the larger experience but will usually affect a smaller number of students. Lacking the generational spectrum within the community, campus ministers need to be alert to incorporating those missing elements into sermons and other programs. On campus, the church community has a special need to reach out to the world which is rarely a part of campus life.

PRESENCE

Through campus ministry, the church is present in an environment which often does not judge it to be necessary or even sometimes welcome. Aside from Catholic and other explicitly religious colleges and universities, few university administrators would purposefully create a Catholic campus ministry, if it were absent, although most will welcome its presence as long as it is supported and funded by the church. On the scale of priorities, religious ministry would not loom very high for most presidents and administrators. This attitude is not so much one of hostility but rather an indifference born of the widespread notion that religious activity is only a highly personal private affair, best left to each individual's private tastes.

Thus, the very presence of a Catholic faith community on campus is radically different from the presence of a parish in a town or city where it is assumed and expected. Our presence on a secular campus speaks strongly of the care which the church has for the future, for young people and for the university itself. Campus ministers need to reflect on that presence, how it functions and what it communicates to the whole campus community. While it is obvious that the existence of a community of faith should be well known to prospective members through advertising, outreach and other contact, it is also important that it be known to those who, while not seeking membership, can gain an appreciation of the vitality of religious faith on the modern campus.

Increasingly, colleges and universities have established an office or liaison with all the various religious ministries seeking to work on campus. On many campuses there is a semi-professional organization of these ministers with binding rules about proselytizing and the competence of religious workers. Such groupings obviously provide for inter-faith and ecumenical opportunities as well as coordinating many of the practical problems of scheduling the use of chapels and other facilities, and for planning joint speaker and seminar programs. Yet these organizations do not supply the dynamism for Catholic ministry which arises from the inner life of the church and its sacramental life of worship.

Presence requires visibility. Catholic ministry must be public, addressing the issues of the university in ways that can be known by the larger campus community. Use and access to the campus press, contact with other student organizations, participation (when welcomed) in university ceremonies and sheer physical visibility on campus all make our presence real.

Presence also requires availability, readiness and a welcoming spirit. Student conversations are full of horror stories, real or exaggerated, about the unavailability of deans, administrators or professors. Even the smaller institutions can be uncommonly bureaucratic and replete with endless red tape. Trying to get beyond the secretary guarding the door, or waiting for a form to be signed by the proper official, or figuring out what the requirements of a program really mean can daunt even the most intelligent and persistent students.

Campus ministers and their office arrangements should seek to avoid the appearance of such university mazes. While there has to be some scheduling and no one can be in two places at the same time, we need to be creative in our efforts to be available, approachable and, simply, easy to reach. The sheer physical reality of being on the campus is a key. If we allow ourselves to be drawn away to too many other activities, or allow meetings to make us physically present but unavailable, the perception quickly grows among students that we are just another inaccessible campus figure. Some campus ministers find it very useful to be seen frequently in the student union or cafeteria or other student hang-outs where a message of availability can be clearly communicated. Likewise, having an office that gains the reputation for being open and welcoming gives the same message. Showing up at lectures and other campus programs promotes the sense that we are here and available. Presence and availability plant seeds. It does not mean that every time a campus minister is seen having coffee in the student union someone will come over for an important conversation, but it does mean that many students passing by will notice and file away in their minds that message of availability for future use.

At the same time, campus ministers need to have a sense of the "students' turf" and respect the privacy of places where adult presence is not generally welcomed. Dormitories, other living situations, and many social events do not provide a good venue, unless we are there for a very specific purpose. Inappropriate presence can readily be perceived as snooping or intrusion.

CENTERED YET PRESENT

The inherent temptation in campus ministry is to over-value relevance and the fads of the present moment. There is great cultural pressure on campus to be "with it" and to be "now." Ironically, one of the strongest attractions of the Catholic tradition on campus is that it does not usually present itself as a prisoner of the present moment but, while it takes the present moment with profound seriousness and attention, it also points to a time long ago when the Word became flesh, and looks to a time in an unseen future when "all things will be restored in Christ." Rarely are campus ministers pulled in the direction of the timeless; more frequently the demand is to become fully absorbed in what presents itself now.

We need to resist the allure of being reinvented by the demands of the moment. Chesterton's insight speaks to the experience of campus ministry. "He who marries the spirit of the age will soon find himself a widower." Sociologist Peter Berger offers the warning as a challenge: "Christians who consider themselves progressives [said a Spanish sociologist] always tell us to 'read the signs of the times'; has it never occurred to these people that they might write some of these signs."

In fact Catholic campus ministry is writing one of the most powerful signs of this era by gathering communities of faith and worship in the midst of the most secularized environments of our time. That this is happening on college campuses is one of the least understood opportunities in the church today, but it is surely a sign being written in our times.

A short generation ago, at the Second Vatican Council, the momentous contribution which the American church made to the church universal was the lived experience of religious liberty and the confidence that, in a free society, the church could thrive and fulfill its mission. Today, the contribution of the church in this allegedly most secular of cultures may well be to demonstrate the vitality of the gospel in the midst of the secularist enclaves of higher education. As Marxism in the east was revealed to have utterly failed in its effort to purge the spiritual and Christian dimensions of human life, so secularism has failed to banish that same Spirit to the hidden recesses of a purely private oblivion.

Among the young, especially on campus, there is a readiness for the work of that Spirit.

THE PARISH MODEL

At many larger universities, campus ministry is often part of a university parish which serves the campus as well as those who live nearby. University parishes can more easily avoid some of the limitations I discussed earlier because they usually involve people of diverse generations and needs. At the University of California at Berkeley, where I served for a number of years, a large university parish ministered to a vast range and diversity of people. The richness and full scope of the church can be more readily embodied in this type of campus ministry. But it can also be very large, with many Sunday liturgies and an array of programs which make it difficult to know people very well. In these parishes there is always the looming danger of overlooking the students who attend because they do not become as active in parish affairs as residential parishioners and because the students are not there for significant periods of the year during which the parish continues its life. One remedy that is increasingly utilized is to assign some members of the parish staff to be primarily or exclusively concerned with student and campus ministry. Another effort to avoid letting students get lost in the shuffle is to structure some student involvement in each parish activity or program, e.g. setting aside student seats on the parish council and other committees.

Invariably, at campus parishes, one or more of the Sunday liturgies will tend to become a "student mass" because of the time of day and the style of the liturgy. Despite all the other demands of a busy university parish, it is important to give priority to this liturgy, especially in terms of building a sense of community among the students and providing a measure of the sense of "ownership" which I described earlier.

Other colleges and universities, like the one where I now serve, will not have a parish-based campus ministry, but, over the years, geography and demographics will have created a ministry that is not parish-based but relies on its own less structured presence on campus. Many of the usual parish structures and strengths will be lacking but it has the opportunity to be more directly student-and campus-oriented in its focus, energy and programs. Here the campus minister will have to create, to a large extent, his or her role on campus, and, as a result, there is a great variety of campus ministry models depending on the specific configurations of each school. Commuter schools, residential colleges, community colleges and ones in the midst of town-gown conflict will all inspire very different models of campus ministry.

In all these ministries, however, the campus ministers need to be constantly casting a glance at the parish model, not because they should be trying to duplicate it, but because it does flesh out the whole of the church's ministry and can serve as landmark, occasionally reminding us of what we are tending to overlook or neglect when our ministry is focused exclusively on students and the campus.

The university parish and the non-parish-based campus ministry complement each other in ways which underline the importance of ministers from both models meeting and sharing their experiences. Each campus is so unique that we frequently turn off our attention when we hear about a very different campus, thinking that there is little to be gained from a radically different set-up. At this point we need to be reminded that our ministry is rooted in the church's presence and not created by the specifics of our campus. Each campus is very different, but in some very important ways the ministry is common—the proclamation of the gospel, the celebration of the sacraments and the gathering of the faith community.

AFTER GRADUATION

"It's just not the same as it was at school." "The sermons are so awful." "I go every now and then but I just feel so strange because I don't know anybody there." "Do you know of any parish in _____ (fill in the name of any city) like the one we had at school."

At a wedding reception, at homecoming, at the funeral of a former student's parent, at almost any occasion where I meet former students, I hear these familiar reasons for not attending mass the way they did at college. Obviously I have not been circulating around, asking those present if they still attend mass. They bring it up, right away, because it is really bothering them. Former students for whom mass and their religion were very much a part of their lives in college miss it. They haven't done much about it, but they feel it and want to have their faith alive again. They are mostly single, job- or grad-school oriented, and finding they do not fit into parish life.

"You people give these kids such an unreal experience on campus." "These young people come here thinking they're going to find the closeness of a Newman Center. We can't provide that. We have a couple of thousand people, a school and a hospital plus three nursing homes." "You've got a great luxury over there on campus. You can get to know every kid. You don't have the pressure we have here in a parish."

Now I am at a social gathering of pastoral associates and priests from the local parishes. They want me to understand that campus ministers are not preparing students for the realities of a real-life parish. They fully understand the problem of young single Catholics not finding a home in the parish, but they tend to think it is because, on campus, we promise too much.

It is all true and we are all right. There is a problem. And none of us—students, graduates, campus ministers and parish ministers—are doing enough to make the transition from campus to the real-world parish an inviting prospect for young Catholics. And what we are doing, we are not yet doing together.

In the final chapter, I will suggest ten ways in which all of us in the church could work to deepen the faith life of those who move on from our campus communities after college and who could be the greatest resource for the vitality of tomorrow's parish. These ten suggestions will not be new or startling, but perhaps, reviewing them together, we can begin to create a new dynamic in the life of the church, on campus and in the parish. However, before we start listing ways out of the dilemma we need to examine the dilemma—and its immense opportunity—in more detail

To the larger church, especially parishes and diocesan ministries, campus ministers bring a crucial message, perhaps in the form of a revelation. Young people in our society are quite religious and will respond in significant numbers and with enthusiasm to the church's ministry and worship. Catholic campus ministers on nearly every American campus can bear witness to this phenomenon that challenges the complacent writing-off of young people, which is not uncommon among pastoral workers.

At the same time we have yet another message for the church which details the fall-off in religious practice that frequently occurs when students graduate and move on from campus communities. Part of this change in religious practice can be understood in terms of their sudden transition into the dislocation of modern working or job seeking, moving to strange and new places for the sake of a job or graduate school, and the loss of the sense of all their communities, including their religious one, when college ends. Partially, it must also be admitted, we have created an artificially high level of expectation for religious community with the smaller more personal faith gatherings that are typically offered on campus and that cannot be realistically expected in "the real world." But some part of the explanation for the fall-off in religious practice is also the neglect which our parishes often exhibit toward the young, especially the young who are still single. Wander through a typical American parish on a Sunday morning, glance at the bulletin and the posters which advertise programs and activities, listen to the examples that are used in sermons and to the announcements made at mass. With the exception of some things offered to senior citizens, nearly everything will be focused on families, on couples with children, on school or other youth activities. When we visually imagine the make-up of a parish in a large metropolitan area, we do not routinely include in that vision the up to one-fifth of its residents who are young, between the ages of twenty-two and thirty, single, and working and/or in graduate school. The marriage age has been moving to the late twenties among this group, making them single for often nearly a decade, as they move frequently and live quite anonymously in our midst. A prevailing wisdom tells us that they are not very religious anyhow—the same prevailing wisdom that depicts college students as hopelessly non-religious.

However, there is no substantial reason to accept this

view. What the public opinion polls tells us about this population can be readily confirmed by campus ministers. In great numbers, they are believers, they pray, and they seek to be part of a community which shares these beliefs. Of course, they could all just show up in large numbers in our parishes and by their sheer presence create a new focus for the parish. But people are not like that, and, young or old, they look for invitations, words of welcome, signs that they will feel at home. Often not living in one neighborhood or town for very long, young people are doubly reluctant to assert their presence or their needs at a local parish. The nearly universal experience of Catholic campus ministers shows that we are missing something, or, more accurately, we are missing someone, young, single and Catholic, in our parishes. And very frequently that missing person was very much a part of a worshiping community a few months or a few years ago.

THE WELL-BEING AND WHOLENESS OF A CAMPUS MINISTER

Ministry burnout happens in campus ministry, perhaps more frequently than in other forms of ministry. People get frustrated, lose interest, become tired and, most of all, simply lose patience. Students and others involved in campus communities are usually the first to notice when a campus minister seems to lose heart or become distracted. More than perhaps in any other area of church life, a campus community has to minister to the minister. The friendship, support and the challenge of the congregation is essential to the well-being of a campus minister. Understanding the special pressures of campus ministry can help the community to provide strong support for its ministers.

Campus ministers need to devote some of their time

alone, and together with other campus ministers, to their own development and well-being. The frenetic activity of campus life can be a very dangerous current, especially with its quixotic patterns of speeding up when the semester begins and then coming to a dramatic halt when school closes up for a break or vacation. One day a campus minister may have thirty things to do, and the next day have nothing to do because the campus is shut tight as a drum.

Time is an unpredictable element. Late night calls, unscheduled requests for time, emergencies that turn out not to be emergencies, and some emergencies that involve life and death make the neat schedule a rarity. Some limits have to be set, including regular time off and away from the campus. Many campus ministers find it useful to follow the practice of doctors and other professionals by calling people who have made appointments the day before to double check that they are still intending to keep that appointment. Pulling together some group discussions around personal issues can not only lessen the time demands for personal counseling but actually often produce more effective results. Knowing when you are too tired or too drained, and admitting that to oneself, is always the most reliable safeguard.

Many campus ministers have other pastoral duties which can include a part-time regular parish ministry elsewhere. Trying to keep these duties and locales separate can help lessen the running back and forth both physically and emotionally. Days or parts of days clearly devoted to each can set some boundaries which people in both communities usually come to recognize and respect. Utilizing contemporary telephone technology can broaden our availability while reducing the strain of being constantly but inefficiently in motion.

Most campus ministers spend a good deal of time with students, much of it social time, while usually being at least one or two generations older than the students. Students relish this closeness and camaraderie and in many cases campus ministers are among the few adults with whom they have close contact. Nearly every campus minister will rate highly this access of students to their time and company. It is also very rewarding. Yet campus ministers will try to find the balance of being approachable and friendly without succumbing to the illusion that they are just one of the student gang. In fact, students will be curtly dismissive of any adult, especially a campus minister, who tries too hard, or too falsely, to be one of them. They expect us to act our age because that is what is of value to them in their closeness with us.

In this age of yearly evaluation forms and meetings, we all laugh at the jargon-filled questions directed at us. How is your job satisfaction? Leaving aside the bureaucratic jargon, the question is always to the point. Do I enjoy my work? Do I merely endure it, just waiting for something I might like? Does this role of campus minister create too much stress? Temperamentally some people are wrongly placed in this ministry, while others thrive on it. However we fill out the evaluation forms, we need to be very clear with ourselves, and ultimately with our superiors, about our enjoyment and fulfillment in this ministry. If we are not suited for this, it will first become evident to everyone around us, and then will drain us of our spirit. Effective campus ministers have to enjoy the campus milieu, students and their foibles, and the less structured pastoral environment, and they have to enjoy most of what they are called to do each day. Answering the question of job satisfaction, at least to our own satisfaction, is essential to our well-being and wholeness.

Related to job satisfaction is accountability, not in the sense of being constantly checked on but in the sense being part of a larger mission. Too many campus ministers feel they are off by themselves, alone and without support. If some structured accountability with its attendant support is not provided, we can reach out for it to someone in the diocese, in our religious community, in the local parish or to a group of colleagues who can help to provide it. Being unsupervised is a most illusory freedom which quickly degenerates into feeling uncared for.

Judgment is the most requisite quality for the well-being of a campus minister. In a ministry without many precedents or procedures in place, the judgment of the campus minister is paramount. Negotiating the delicate antagonisms of the many interest groups on campus claiming our attention, dealing with emotionally charged student problems and student-faculty encounters, navigating the personality conflicts that loom large in the small world of academe, and constantly engaging in one-to-one dealing with usually close congregations—all demand intuitive and quick judgment. Experience sharpens that judgment and the experience of other campus ministers can add great value to our own experience. The strain of making these judgments is always lessened when we first talk it over with people we trust and in collaboration with those who may share our responsibility.

Larger universities will usually have a campus ministry team of a number of people working in a collaborative model together. All the dynamics of collaborative ministry at work now throughout the church will come to bear on this process. Division of labor, mutual respect and open consultation are here on campus, as everywhere, the hallmarks of successful team ministry. The struggle and effort to engage each other in collaborative ministry is never without its price, even as it produces great fulfillment and satisfaction. On campus there are many resources to aid the growth of team ministry, including outside facilitators and group workers who can bring a wealth of skill to our efforts. Our reaching out to these professionals on campus for assistance often unknowingly opens up whole new avenues in our outreach to the university.

The mutuality of care for well-being and wholeness between a community and its ministers is more obvious and direct in campus faith communities where it is also more possible and more required. Neither the community nor its ministers can thrive without the giving and receiving of this care. Its absence or interruption can be destructive. But when it flourishes, as it often does, it also serves as an invaluable model of the church which, not least among its many assets, is remarkably successful in bringing about what we aspire to signify about the Christian mystery of life together, on earth, as it is in heaven and on campus.

11

Ten Guidelines to Help Young People Deepen Their Faith Life after College

On graduation morning, the air is filled with celebration. The campus is filled with crowds and music. The sound of congratulations is everywhere. Parents, grandparents and friends pack the whole quad, cameras in hand, ready to celebrate one of our society's most important rites of passage.

But when the ceremonies are over and I move through the crowds to congratulate the seniors, I often see tears in their eyes. Now in the midst of all the relief that it is over and all the feelings of accomplishment and anticipation, there is also the sad realization that something unique and wonderful is now coming to an end, something that will never be repeated again in life. It is time to move on.

Recognizing the difficulties of this transition, the university has been providing an array of resources to these seniors for the past year: career and academic counseling, seminars and workshops on how to make the adjustment and, at the very end, a senior week full of social activities to help cement the friendships and relationships that have been formed these past four years.

Campus ministry needs to take a cue from these efforts and to realize that we can also help students from our campus faith communities make the transition to the larger church, usually the parish, and set out for them some things to look for. We do this also because now men and women we have known as college students have the potential to bring that faith and vitality into thousands of parishes every year.

In the guidelines that follow, you will find much common sense and accepted wisdom. Students who review them all together before they leave their campus faith community will have a clearer sense of how to bridge their faith life on campus with that of the real world. Campus ministers who make a point of surveying these guidelines in their farewells to graduating students will greatly prepare the way for a new vitality in the whole church.

Perhaps most useful would be the coming together of parish ministers and campus ministers, in a region or a diocese, to review these guidelines, add their own, and try to integrate the difficult process of transition into both campus ministry and parish ministry. These guidelines, along with some other suggestions, could take the form of a brochure or letter sent to graduating seniors as a congratulations message from their campus ministers. A similar brochure or letter could be offered, either personally or through a mailing, by the parish as it consciously welcomes these new young people into their parish each year. Diocesan offices of campus ministry might hold a workshop for parish ministers to help them understand and engage these newly graduated students in their parishes. They are easily overlooked, or wrongly assumed to be non-religious, when they are an enormous resource waiting to be welcomed by our parishes and other ministries.

When it comes time to move on . . .

1. FIND A PARISH

The next place where you worship will probably not be as convenient as the Newman Center or campus chapel was in college. But neither will cafeterias and bookstores and friends be just a few steps away from where you are going to live or work. And parishes can be very different, based on their location, the needs and age of the congregation, and, of course, the parish staff. Look around your new location, ask some Catholics you admire where they worship, talk to some priests or pastoral workers who will understand what you are looking for. Even in the same parish, liturgies can be very different, and you may find that an evening mass or a folk mass gathers a more lively and welcoming congregation. Don't allow yourself to be quickly put off just by large numbers, but realize that a congregation that looks huge is always composed of smaller groupings and communities.

Worshiping communities also gather at colleges or downtown centers, and even though you are new to the area, you may find a very inviting community in places other than the usual parish.

Most importantly, look for a parish or worshiping community where you could give something of your time and yourself. The needs may be very different from those you knew at college, but many parishes could greatly benefit from your time and skill in their social action programs, homeless shelter or food pantry, or with kids in their school, in their youth ministry program or with senior citizens. Offer to help with the music at a liturgy on Sundays, especially if it seems to be one that you would like to identify with. The religious education program in the parish would probably be delighted to have the help of a recent college graduate. Offer to teach or lead a group in their high school religious education program. Contact the parish youth minister and make yourself available to help teenagers. Suggest to the parish staff the formation of a parish-wide group of recent, young and single college graduates. Be sure to publicize the group in town newspapers and with flyers left at social hangouts and health clubs where it might be seen by people like yourself who are not yet involved in the parish.

If the parish seems to leave a lot to be desired, see that as meaning that it still has plenty of room for new life and new people like yourself and people your age. If there seem to be very few young people in church on Sunday, become a parish leader and make the parish aware. Give some of yourself to the parish and, unless you meet some peculiar resistance, you will quickly get things done. If you make this a priority, your new parish will very quickly become your parish community and a central dimension of your new life.

2. LEARN MORE ABOUT YOUR FAITH

Remember all the books you put off reading until you had the time after graduation and all the extra skills you planned to acquire when you were out from under the pressure of college life? Now is also the time to deepen the knowledge of your faith. In most dioceses there are extensive adult education programs in scripture, moral theology and liturgical expertise. Sometimes these are offered right in the parish, but often they are available at centers or retreat houses around the diocese. Make a few phone calls, get their brochures or catalogues, and look for a course or workshop that interests you. You will keep your faith alive, and you will meet people like yourself who are interested in spiritual and personal growth.

Many parishes have small Bible study groups, or prayer groups, or groups formed around personal growth issues. In these groups you see the vast parish congregation break down into manageable gatherings of real people whose names you will know. Get involved in one of these groups and, like volunteering, it will quickly make the huge Sunday crowd look friendlier because you will know many of its members.

If you look beyond the parish, you will find courses in religious education offered by the diocese to prepare teachers of religion. Get some technique and expertise in this area and then work with the children or teenagers in the parish. You will see the wealth of programs in religious education in today's church, and you will also be making yourself a skilled teacher of religion for the children you may have yourself in the future.

If you still have some academic interests from your college years, check out the credit courses in theology and scripture at the area Catholic colleges. Most of them are arranged especially for people pursuing a master's degree part-time, and you might discover the whole world of theology and advanced scripture study. At these same schools, look into degree programs that could work in tangent with your job or future professional plans, like medical ethics, business ethics or social justice. Talk with people in these programs, and as you deepen and enrich your own faith life, you may even open up some new career possibilities for yourself.

3. PREPARE FOR MARRIAGE

If you are now in a serious relationship, marriage is already something you have been thinking about, at least remotely. And even if you are not now involved with someone, you undoubtedly think about serious relationships and marriage. Yet marriage is a bit scary for most today. There are all the ominous divorce statistics and you probably know some contemporaries who have already gone through the marriage and divorce rituals. Many of us today have had divorces in our own families with our parents or brothers and sisters. It is all more than a bit intimidating, but yet almost everyone aspires to a good and fulfilling marriage that will work and last.

Nowhere is marriage taken with more seriousness, of course, than the Catholic Church, but even the church does not have a fail-safe book or program to guarantee a good marriage. In nearly every diocese and parish now, however, there are marriage preparation programs (sometimes still called "Pre-Cana") which provide engaged couples with some excellent insights and experience by which they can deepen the communication and commitment they already have. Some couples seeking marriage are put off and annoyed when they are asked to take a marriage preparation course, often naively thinking that they have already worked out all their potential problems or romantically believing that love conquers all difficulties. But even those couples who attend marriage preparation programs with obvious reluctance usually come away from them as enthusiastic fans.

Most programs are conducted by a team of married couples with a priest and focus on communication skills and difficulties, the experience of married couples, and a view of the spirituality of marriage as a sacrament. Some programs are held in parishes on a series of evenings, others are weekend programs. I strongly urge couples to do the Engaged Encounter Weekend, but caution them to make a reservation early because the word of mouth popularity of these weekends usually fills them up early. Rarely in ministry is anything one hundred percent, but I can testify to the near one hundred percent enthusiasm which couples have for these weekends, even those who went with some reluctance or trepidation.

As you look to marriage, however close or remote that might be for you now, see the marriage preparation experi-

162   College Catholics

ence as at least as important as all the other social and cultural things which surround marriage in our culture. Make it
an integral part of your wedding and see it as an important
sign of the seriousness with which you will enter into your
marriage.

4. JOIN OR FORM A SMALL CHRISTIAN COMMUNITY

Everywhere Christians are gathering in smaller, more personal groups to get beyond the size and anonymity that can
mark congregational life. Often parish-based but also spring-
ing up in many other contexts, these groups sometimes focus
on specific tasks like social justice or a simpler living style, or
they have no specific issue, but are an opportunity for people
to share the Christian life more intimately. Some of these
small groups live together for a community experience, while
others meet once a week or monthly in some common place.
There are such groups especially geared to newly married
couples, just as there are many that mainly appeal to single
people.

Consider becoming involved in a group that meets your
schedule, your lifestyle and your needs. Again you may have
to look around or ask around, but you will find such groups
everywhere. If not, invite a few people who share your faith
to join with you in starting a small Christian community. Start
small and low-key and let it evolve to meet the real needs of
the participants. Integrate the group into your parish life, or
relate it to the place where you are working, or peg it to a
specific issue like being single or concerned about drug addiction and recovery, or just gather some people in your neighborhood or housing complex.

Small Christian communities are filling a great need in
the contemporary church and may be the way for you to

anchor your faith life in a deep inter-personal bonding with other people having the same faith perspective.

5. DEEPEN YOUR PRAYER LIFE

In the months or years after graduation, more than a few frustrations and difficulties will have led you to pray. If you are like the ninety percent of college students whom I described earlier in the book and who answered my surveys by citing "prayer" as the main reason for their participation in worship, then prayer is already important in your life. Like most of us, you do it all the time.

Now away from a campus community with which you were able to share your prayer life and feel the closeness of that community, you may have to search out some new opportunities for your prayer experience. Prayer groups now gather in the most amazing places. Early every morning one prayer group meets quietly in the White House, another in the U.S. Senate, others in IBM offices and among firemen in the local firehouse. Often ecumenical and very open to different forms of prayer, these groups appeal to our need to set aside some time, however brief, to be with others and God. If there is no group now where you work or live, see if you can get one started. Just invite a few friendly believers to pray together.

Retreats were probably a major part of your campus faith community. Make a retreat this year. There are so many thriving retreat houses everywhere because the demand is so great. Some retreats are geared to specific groups—women, men, single, married, youth, people coping with a loss, people in recovery, people with nearly every kind of interest or need. You can get information about all the local retreat houses and their programs from your parish or from the diocesan offices.

If you have a more contemplative bent, seek out a local monastery. Most of them have guest houses where you can spend some time, sharing in their liturgy and sharing in the timeless prayer life of monastic men or women.

6. UNLOCK THE RICHES OF THE BIBLE

Prayer leads us to that formidable book, the Bible. Aside from the readings we hear at mass, most of us have little contact with this paramount source of the Christian life. The Bible is intimidating and we all smile a bit when we hear someone announce plans to read the Bible cover to cover. In fact, that is not a very good way to get into the Bible. We need some background and some skills before we can find our way around the book and unlock its riches.

Just in our diocese alone, I know of dozens of excellent short courses being offered on the Bible, usually in parishes or downtown centers. These courses focus on one book or one section of the Bible, providing an excellent introduction and an in-depth understanding. In the church today there are many very talented and proficient teachers of the Bible who know how to open up the book and engage our fascination. You will easily find a course or seminar like this, and it will unfold the enjoyment and nourishment provided by modern biblical studies.

You can also make the Bible a part of your own personal prayer life each day. Take one book, like the Psalms or the Gospel of John, and read a short section each day. Let yourself dwell on a few of the words and let the words take your imagination where they will. Don't read too much or devour it like a best-seller. Just let a few verses each day work through your consciousness and let them speak to you.

Like many people today, you may also find great value in

sharing that experience with others in some regular Bible study group. People take some passages and see how they illuminate their lives and the concerns that are shared by the group.

Depending on your time and interests, you will find an array of Bible study opportunities, from the academic to the very personal, and will see how they contribute to your faith life.

7. EXPAND YOUR KNOWLEDGE OF CHRISTIAN CULTURE

A fine arts professor on this campus leads a student group to Italy every spring break to visit Rome, Florence and Venice. The emphasis of the trip is on his specialty, art and architecture, and all students who make the trip point to it as one the best things they did in college. The Catholic students who make the trip also tell me how much this encounter with great Christian art has personally enhanced their appreciation of their faith and its meaning.

The worlds of art, music, literature, film and theater, from the very classical to the contemporary, are a fascinating place in which your faith can be reflected through the brilliant insights and experiences of others. Perhaps you have a strong interest in one of these areas already, or have been planning to learn more when you have the time. You can combine your cultural interests with your faith life and bring a fresh perspective to both.

A new exhibition or a series of lectures at the local or university museum on an era or artist, exploring the experience of belief or unbelief, can enrich your imagination as well as your faith life. See about getting a group in your parish to meet together before visiting the museum to educate itself and discuss the project. An event like this will bring new people into parish life. If your interests in culture are strong, check out the graduate courses available in your area. Consider forming a group to read great literature or attend the theater and then have discussions about the personal impact of these works.

Modern films often explore the issues of faith and how people struggle with hope and despair. Some films, like *Black Robe* and *The Mission,* also reach back into Christian history. Certain directors, like Martin Scorcese and Ingmar Bergman, are renowned for their explorations in film of life's great questions. Today a film festival can be as easy as putting a cassette into a VCR and requires little cost. Nearly everyone loves films, and it is easy to gather people to discuss the impact of a film. A film series is yet another excellent way of having a parish show its welcome and hospitality to young people.

New areas are opening up all the time. Just now, for example, the end of communism in the former Soviet Union has unleashed a great outpouring of interest in the great religious icons of Russia. Invite a Russian Orthodox priest or scholar to give a presentation to your group about the historic significance of icons in Russia. The growing significance of Islam on the world stage is drawing many people to study the art and literature of the Moslem peoples. Have an evening presentation on the history and art of Islam with a scholar from the field.

Drawing people together to reflect on the intersections of religion and culture will bring some fascinating people into your group, parish or other activity. Usually these stimulating gatherings lead to many other plans and activities.

Pilgrims may not be traveling on foot to the great shrines and places of faith these days, but today there are more pilgrims than ever in history. Travel can be a renewal of the soul as well as a vacation. Look into some of the tours to historic places in Europe, South America and the Holy Land which emphasize the Christian heritage of these countries. Often these tours are so efficiently organized that they can offer trips at a cost far less than regular travel. Don't hesitate to go on one of these tours alone, if your vacation does not coincide with your friends' time off, because you will meet other people and enjoy the time away, in addition to all you will see and learn.

8. BE INVOLVED IN SOCIAL JUSTICE CONCERNS

The modern church is strongly attentive to the injustice and suffering still so prevalent in society and throughout the world. Given all the teachings of the pope and the American bishops and the experience of so many Catholics in the third world (at home and abroad), it is pretty hard to take seriously a Catholic who is not also committed to social justice—and doing something about it. And people are doing something about it. Poverty, homelessness, the environment, the Pro-Life movement and other areas of social reform have legions of committed Catholics and other Christians involved. All these issues have surely crossed your mind and you have thought of ways of doing your part. See your activity as an extension of your faith, whether or not the group you work with is explicitly religious or not.

None of us can do or change everything, so we need to choose our involvement carefully and realistically. Find a group or organization that is focused on an area of your interest, or one that can use your skills. Make a commitment, but be clear to yourself and the others about the time you have. Some groups work very directly with the legislative process and other parts of the established system, others are more widely educational; some concentrate on fund-raising, while still others meet needs directly, getting involved with soup kitchens and homeless shelters. Your own temperament, philosophy and time constraints will be your guide.

Like most involved and committed people, you will soon be saying that you are getting a lot more out of what you're doing than what you're giving. And you will be giving reality and flesh to the great insight of the modern church that social justice is a constitutive element of the gospel.

9. BECOME A VOLUNTEER

Nowhere is it written in stone that college graduates have to move on immediately into graduate school or a dream job. In fact, the reality today is that there are few dream jobs around, and more and more graduate schools prefer to admit people who have some years of work or other experience after college. For these and other reasons, many college seniors today consider giving a year or two of their life as a volunteer. Interest in the Peace Corps has been picking up in recent years. Hundreds of volunteer programs are also connected with religious organizations, working here at home and overseas. Time spent as a volunteer provides people with a rare experience, gives them the added time to figure out their long-term goals, and does a lot of good for other people. Doing something like this for a year or two may have already crossed your mind. There are some excellent resources to help you decide.

Call or write the nearest Pallotti Center, a clearing house of endless information about volunteer opportunities, often associated with religious organizations. The staff at a Pallotti Center can help you find opportunities that fit your needs and interests. They also publish a very complete handbook with descriptions of many of these opportunities. The Jesuit

Volunteer Corps is one of the largest and best opportunities and emphasizes the community and spiritual life of those working together. But there are hundreds of others to be looked at, some associated with Catholic religious orders and groups, some which are ecumenical, and some which are specialized to certain regions, like Appalachia or the inner city. The Catholic Worker Movement has houses of hospitality, food and clothing programs, and even farms which serve the needs of the poorest among us. Many dioceses have recently organized a volunteer program where people work on a parish staff for a year or two. Talk to some people already in these programs to get a better sense of what is involved. Ask your campus minister, since he or she will likely have known many students who have served as volunteers.

If you are considering something more like a career than a stint as a volunteer, look into the excellent work of Catholic Relief Services which is the largest, worldwide, non-governmental aid and development agency. Or bring your skills, and career plans, to the various agencies of Catholic Charities, which is a vast service network, second only to the government in the help it provides to people in need.

Even if right now you are thinking that a volunteer opportunity is just something to do before you get a real job or go to grad school, or just something that might look good on your resume, look into it. You may be surprised that it will do those things and much more for you—and for other people.

10. BECOME A WITNESS IN THE WORLD

These suggestions are not meant to be an exhaustive list of things that will deepen your faith after graduation, although by now it may seem like an exhausting list. Only a few of these suggestions may be relevant to you and your situation. But you get the idea. Just as it would be a tragedy to terminate your general education on graduation day, so it would be a sad loss to let your faith life linger once you have moved on. You have already discovered the power of faith to be an anchor and a challenge during college, now you need your imagination, and some suggestions, to make sure that develops along with the rest of your life.

Out in the "real world," you will be a witness to that faith, bringing the Christian vision to your job, to your marriage, to others, and to healing the world's ills. Far from proselytizing or pushing religion, you are simply demonstrating in your life the connections between your faith and what you do. And, as you already have seen, people become curious about what that connection is. Some, in time, will want that for themselves and ask you about it.

Being a witness also changes the world, in real terms. Looking over all the astounding things that people do to improve the world, it is inescapable that so many of these efforts are religiously based. Indeed, as you move away from the purely theoretical approaches to social change to the more direct ones that actually feed and clothe people, save children from urban horrors, and get things done, you see that these are almost all religiously based. "God is in the details," as the great architect, Mies van der Rohe, said, and nowhere are those details more crucial than when they help other people, often making the difference between life and death.

The blending of Christian faith with the skills and learning you have acquired is now a life project. Whether in politics, in family life, in culture, in race relations, or in international efforts, you will find the unlimited possibility of being that kind of witness.

*   *   *

Campus ministry and campus faith communities are rightly situated at the beginning of a journey because most of those involved are at the beginning of their journey in life. No one knows the future, but we can prepare the ground and prepare ourselves. Sometimes we never get to know the outcome of these journeys, but every now and then we get a glimpse. A few months ago, by mere chance, I heard on my car radio a BBC interview with a doctor who is now working with the victims of the unspeakable horrors of the war in Somalia. At first his name meant nothing to me, a common sounding Irish-American name you hear frequently. But gradually, as the interviewer was drawing out this doctor's inner motivation for working now in Somalia and before that in Ethiopia, I realized that the doctor was a student I had known as an undergraduate in my first campus assignment in the late 1960s. I was only certain of this when I heard the doctor tracing his present work back to his college days when he was active with a group of students from the Catholic campus community who were volunteers at a clinic in one of the poorest neighborhoods in Detroit. I remembered that he often talked about his plans to go on to medical school, but I am quite certain that I never saw him again after graduation. As I listened to the interview, I was stuck in the kind of horrendous traffic backup which can only happen on Storrow Drive in Boston, but the wonder of accidentally hearing about this former student on a random BBC interview negated even that frustration. That night I wrote to the doctor, in care of the Catholic agency he was working with, not even sure that he would remember the rookie priest chaplain of his undergraduate days.

About a month later, I received a long letter from him, describing the life which he, his wife and three children, have followed for the past thirteen years among the war victims of the Horn of Africa. And he did remember, in amazing detail,

all the people and events that had been part of that small
Catholic community on an urban commuter campus in Detroit. He reminisced about those days as if they were vividly
present to him now on the other side of the world, in one of
this earth's present horrors. And I know that those experiences in a campus community of faith were present to him
now because I had heard him on radio draw the connections
so vividly and so movingly. Because of these connections—
first formed years ago in a campus community of faith—Jesus
Christ is today in Mogadishu, Somalia, healing the wounded,
touching the forgotten and saving us all again.